P9-CQV-141

# TIME
# Annual 2013

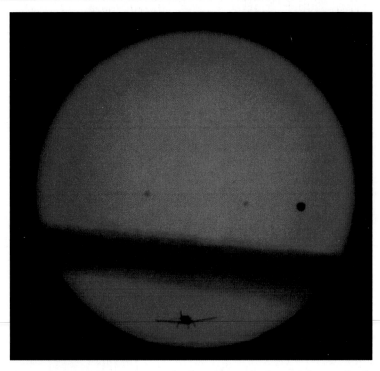

GENE BLEVINS—REUTERS

**Passing through** *On June 5, 2012, the planet Venus, the dot on right, completed a transit across the face of the sun, along with an airplane in this view. If you missed it, patience is advised: the next transit will occur on Dec. 15, 2117*

# TIME

**MANAGING EDITOR** Richard Stengel
**ART DIRECTOR** D.W. Pine
**DIRECTOR OF PHOTOGRAPHY** Kira Pollack

## Annual 2013

**EDITOR** Kelly Knauer
**DESIGNER** Ellen Fanning
**PHOTO EDITOR** Dot McMahon
**ASSISTANT PHOTO EDITOR** Richard Boeth
**RESEARCH** Tresa McBee
**COPY EDITOR** Bruce Christopher Carr

TIME HOME ENTERTAINMENT

**PUBLISHER** Jim Childs
**VICE PRESIDENT, BUSINESS DEVELOPMENT AND STRATEGY** Steven Sandonato
**EXECUTIVE DIRECTOR, MARKETING SERVICES** Carol Pittard
**EXECUTIVE DIRECTOR, RETAIL AND SPECIAL SALES** Tom Mifsud
**EXECUTIVE PUBLISHING DIRECTOR** Joy Butts
**DIRECTOR, BOOKAZINE DEVELOPMENT AND MARKETING** Laura Adam
**FINANCE DIRECTOR** Glenn Buonocore
**ASSOCIATE PUBLISHING DIRECTOR** Megan Pearlman
**ASSISTANT GENERAL COUNSEL** Helen Wan
**ASSISTANT DIRECTOR, SPECIAL SALES** Ilene Schreider
**BOOK PRODUCTION MANAGER** Suzanne Janso
**DESIGN AND PREPRESS MANAGER** Anne-Michelle Gallero
**BRAND MANAGER** Michela Wilde
**ASSOCIATE BRAND MANAGER** Isata Yansaneh
**ASSOCIATE PREPRESS MANAGER** Alex Voznesenskiy

**EDITORIAL DIRECTOR** Stephen Koepp
**EDITORIAL OPERATIONS DIRECTOR** Michael Q. Bullerdick

**SPECIAL THANKS**
Katherine Barnet, Jeremy Biloon, Susan Chodakiewicz, Rose Cirrincione, Lauren Hall Clark, Brian Fellows, Jacqueline Fitzgerald, Christine Font, Jenna Goldberg, Hillary Hirsch, David Kahn, Amy Mangus, Robert Marasco, Kimberly Marshall, Amy Migliaccio, Nina Mistry, Dave Rozzelle, Ricardo Santiago, Adriana Tierno, Vanessa Wu, TIME Imaging

ISBN 10: 1-61893-020-6. ISBN 13: 978-1-61893-020-0. ISSN: 1097-57211

Copyright © 2012 Time Home Entertainment Inc.
Printed in the U.S.A.

Published by TIME Books, an imprint of Time Home Entertainment Inc.
135 West 50th Street, New York, NY 10020

All rights reserved. No part of this book may be reproduced in any form or by any electronic or mechanical means, including information storage and retrieval systems, without permission in writing from the publisher, except by a reviewer, who may quote brief passages in a review. TIME and the Red Border Design are protected through trademark registration in the United States and in the foreign countries where TIME magazine circulates. TIME is a registered trademark of Time Inc.

We welcome your comments and suggestions about TIME Books. Please write to us at:
TIME Books, Attention: Book Editors, P.O. Box 11016, Des Moines, IA 50336-1016
To order any of our hardcover Collector's Edition books, please call us at 1-800-327-6388
Hours: Monday through Friday, 7 a.m.–8 p.m., or Saturday, 7 a.m.–6 p.m., Central Time

ROBERT MARKOWITZ—NASA

**Icons** *Hitching a ride on a NASA 747, the U.S. space shuttle* Enterprise *flies past the Empire State Building on April 27, en route to its new home as part of the Intrepid Sea, Air and Space Museum in New York City*

# Contents

ANDREW QUILTY—OCULI

**Water world** *In this Instagram photo, surging waves driven by Superstorm Sandy plucked a house from the shoreline in Mantoloking, N.J., and moved it 500 yds. into a nearby lake*

# Images
## 2012

SPENCER PLATT—GETTY IMAGES

**L**ike most presidential election years, 2012 was a long slog of finger-pointing, barb-trading, poll-pondering and wall-to-wall political ads. Amid the surfeit of division, the London Olympics came as a thrilling and unifying diversion. It was a year of marvels in science, as physicists found proof of the elusive "God particle," the Higgs boson, and NASA scored a triumph with the Curiosity rover's picture-perfect landing on Mars. The Middle East was volatile: a civil war shattered Syria, and a video created to offend Muslims did just that, touching off anti-U.S. protests. It was neither the best of times nor the worst: it was a time of suspension, when the future held its breath as Americans cast the ballots that would shape the years to come.

**BLESSINGS NEEDED**

*A stone Madonna presides over a scene of horrendous destruction on Tuesday, Oct. 30, in the Breezy Point neighborhood of New York City, perched on a finger of land in the Atlantic Ocean. A fire broke out the night before in the working-class Queens enclave when Super-storm Sandy plowed ashore, and as high winds spread the flames and a strong storm surge hindered fire fighters, more than 110 homes were destroyed. There was a silver lining: every resident survived.*

**Photograph by Frank Franklin II—AP**

CAUSE AND EFFECT

*Inflamed by an incendiary video made in the U.S. about the Prophet Muhammad, Egyptian protesters tear down the American flag at the U.S. embassy compound in Cairo on Sept. 11. The flag was later temporarily replaced with an Islamic banner. Similar protests took place in a number of Muslim nations around the world.*

**Photograph by Halimelshaarani Elshaarani—AFP/Getty Images**

COLLATERAL DAMAGE

*Relatives and mourners pray over the bodies of Abdullah Alrayzar, 23, on left, and Mohammed Abdul Samee, 35, in the village of Marea, Syria, on Sept. 11, 2012. The two civilians were killed when airplanes dispatched by Bashar Assad's regime bombed the village on the outskirts of Aleppo during Syria's increasingly bloody civil war.*

**Photograph by Muhammed Muheisen—AP Images**

**TOUCHDOWN!**

Engineers at the Jet Propulsion Laboratory in Pasadena, Calif., cheer their achievement as they learn that NASA's Curiosity rover has successfully landed on Mars and has begun sending images back to Earth. Launched on Nov. 26, 2011, the car-sized, nuclear-powered explorer landed on Aug. 5, 2012, only 1.5 miles (2.4 km) from its target site after a journey of 350 million miles (563 km).

**Photograph by Bill Ingalls— NASA**

VANITY'S HARBOR?

VANITY'S HARBOR?

*In June, five months after Italian luxury liner* Costa Concordia *ran aground near the island of Giglio off Italy's northwest coast, the ship lies capsized in the island's harbor. Captain Francesco Schettino was accused of steering the craft too close to the shore, simply to show off—and then of deserting it while passengers were still onboard.*

**Photograph by AGF S.R.L.— REX/REX USA**

# Verbatim: Quotes of the Year

"They are overtaking, approaching the wing from the left, from the right, from above. Well done. Beautiful, guys. Cute. They are three months old but already quite big."

**VLADIMIR PUTIN,** Russia's macho President, who donned a flight suit and flew in an ultraglider to introduce young cranes bred in captivity to flying

"If it's a legitimate rape, the female body has ways to try to shut that whole thing down."

**TODD AKIN,** Missouri Republican candidate for the U.S. Senate, describing his opposition to abortion in cases of rape

"There are 47% of the people ... who are dependent upon government, who believe that they are victims ... who believe that they are entitled to health care, to food, to housing, to you-name-it ... These are people who pay no income tax ... My job is not to worry about those people."

**MITT ROMNEY,** GOP presidential candidate, at a private fund raiser in Boca Raton, Fla.

"We knew it was wrong while we were doing it."

**GREGG WILLIAMS,** former defensive coordinator for the New Orleans Saints of the NFL, on running a bounty system that rewarded players for injuring opponents

**"College graduates should not have to live out their 20s in their childhood bedrooms, staring up at fading Obama posters and wondering when they can move out and get going with life."**

**PAUL RYAN,** Republican vice-presidential candidate, at the GOP Convention

CLOCKWISE FROM TOP LEFT: ALEXEY DRUZHININ—AFP/GETTY IMAGES; MANNIE GARCIA/SHEPARD FAIREY—AP; JUSTIN SULLIVAN—GETTY IMAGES; SID HASTINGS—AP

"'Inspire a generation' is our motto. Not necessarily 'Create a generation,' which is what they sometimes get up to in the Olympic Village."

**BORIS JOHNSON,** irrepressible mayor of London, who also made news when he became tangled up on a zip line

**"The people of Egypt, Libya, Yemen and Tunisia did not trade the tyranny of a dictator for the tyranny of a mob."**

**HILLARY CLINTON,** Secretary of State, at a service marking the return of the remains of four Americans killed in an attack on the U.S. consulate in Benghazi, Libya

**"The fact is, I'm gay, always have been, always will be, and I couldn't be any more happy, comfortable with myself, and proud."**

**ANDERSON COOPER,** TV journalist, coming out in a letter to blogger Andrew Sullivan

TOP, FROM LEFT: SASHA MORDOVETS—GETTY IMAGES; TAYLOR HILL—WIREIMAGE/GETTY IMAGES; GEMMA LUZ. BOTTOM, FROM LEFT: PAUL KITAGAKI JR.—ZUMAPRESS.COM; ERIC RISBERG—AP

"Women. They are a complete mystery."

**STEPHEN HAWKING,** Britain's prize-winning theoretical physicist and author, responding to the question "What do you think most about during the day?" in an interview marking his 70th birthday

**"I would rather be in a cycle where people underestimate us. I think it gives us the latitude to go out and make some big bets."**

**MARK ZUCKERBERG,** Facebook CEO, in his first interview since the company's stock plunged after its disappointing initial public offering

"If you were successful, somebody along the line gave you some help ... Somebody helped to create this unbelievable American system that ... allowed you to thrive. Somebody invested in roads and bridges. If you've got a business—you didn't build that. Somebody else made that happen."

**BARACK OBAMA,** President of the U.S., campaigning in Virginia in July

"It's what I came here to do. I'm now a legend."

**USAIN BOLT,** Jamaican sprinter, after winning gold medals in both the 100- and 200-m races at the Olympic Games in London

# People of the Year

## CLINT EASTWOOD

### The Chair Has the Floor

The most unconventional moment of the Republican Convention in Tampa, Fla., was provided by the legendary actor and director Clint Eastwood, 82. Just before Mitt Romney's scheduled acceptance speech, Eastwood appeared onstage, toting a chair. The Man with No Name proceeded to conduct a dialogue with a Man with No Frame: the chair was a stand-in for President Barack Obama. But Eastwood mangled his planned coup de théâtre, stumbling over his repartee and coming off as ill-prepared and crotchety. The bewildering 11-minute appearance was widely criticized: it turned out no one in the Romney campaign had vetted Eastwood's largely improvised remarks, and senior campaign staffers were as surprised as TV viewers at his gambit.

Fortunately for the star, in Hollywood the road to redemption runs straight through the box office. Within weeks, TIME critic Richard Corliss was praising Eastwood's new movie about an aging baseball scout, *Trouble with the Curve,* as "a solid hit."

## AUNG SAN SUU KYI

### The Mandela of Mandalay

Nobel laureate and famed Burmese democracy advocate Aung San Suu Kyi arrived in the U.S. in September and was feted and honored in a number of cities as she traveled the land. On Sept. 19, she received the Congressional Gold Medal, which she was awarded in absentia while under arrest in 2008. The renowned former political prisoner also met privately with President Barack Obama. Suu Kyi, now 67, spent most of two decades imprisoned or kept under house arrest by Burma's thuggish military junta. But she was released in 2010, and the junta has given way to a quasi-civilian government in which she is a ranking member of parliament.

Suu Kyi's U.S. tour came amid an ongoing thaw in her Southeast Asian nation: also in September, the Burmese government released 541 prisoners, 87 of them recognized as political prisoners, in a new round of amnesties. Suu Kyi warned audiences that Burma remains one of the world's most repressive states, and that its journey to becoming a just society will be long.

## FELIX BAUMGARTNER

### The Man Who Fell to Earth

On Oct. 14, Felix Baumgartner, 43, an Austrian skydiver, BASE jumper and all-around daredevil, stepped off a capsule attached to a helium balloon that had carried him 24 miles (39 km) above the earth—and fell to the planet's surface in a descent that took 9 min., 3 sec. After seven years of planning and several weather delays, it's no wonder "Fearless Felix" was elated after he landed—on his feet—in eastern New Mexico, left.

During his descent, the skydiver reached a top speed of 833.9 m.p.h. (1,342 km/h), becoming the first person to break the sound barrier without a vehicle. Baumgartner told TIME, "I have a lot of fears that normal people have. I'm just not scared of heights. In the beginning, I had trouble with the [pressurized] suit. For an hour I was good, but anything longer, I had anxiety ... I had to work with a psychiatrist." When TIME then inquired about deep-sea diving, the Fearless One admitted: "I could never do that."

FROM TOP: JAMES BORCHUCK—TAMPA BAY TIMES/ZUMA PRESS; PAULA BRONSTEIN—GETTY IMAGES; BALAZS GARDI—RED BULL STRATOS/GETTY IMAGES

FROM LEFT: SPLASH NEWS; GABRIEL BOUYS—AFP/GETTY IMAGES; MARCO GROB

## PRINCE HARRY

# A Royal Rascal's Vegas R. and R.

**Just when Britain's royal family was soaring on a fresh wave of popular affection, with uplift provided by the Queen's Diamond Jubilee and the London Olympic Games, Prince Harry made some very poor choices while on a U.S. vacation in August. The blunders of the third in line for the British throne included choosing a very public location, the Wynn Las Vegas Hotel, for his hijinks with a rotating cast of party girls, removing his clothing during a game of "strip billiards" and allowing himself to be photographed in the nude with a female during the match.**

**The royal nonesuch provided the press with endless fodder, as did the subsequent release of highly invasive long-range paparazzi photos of a topless Duchess of Cambridge on vacation with her husband William in France in September. As for Harry, 28: within weeks of his Nevada revels, the prince was dispatched to Afghanistan to engage in a few months of reputation-building.**

## LANCE ARMSTRONG

# Downhill Slide

On Aug. 23, cycling legend and cancer survivor Lance Armstrong, 41, announced he would not contest charges by the United States Anti-Doping Agency (USADA) that he used performance-enhancing drugs and led a doping ring during his career. Armstrong called the process unfair, noting the agency refused to identify the names of the dozen witnesses slated to testify against him.

Days later, the agency opened its files, revealing a wealth of testimony from teammates that Armstrong had led a tight ring of conspirators who actively doped for years. In the weeks that followed, cycling's world governing body stripped Armstrong of his seven Tour de France titles, while sponsors, including Nike, withdrew their support, and Armstrong resigned as chairman of his cancer-awareness charity, Livestrong. For the cyclist, the pain may only have begun; years of lawsuits are likely to follow.

## ZAHA HADID

# A Wizardly Form Giver Makes Her Mark

Iraqi-born, British-based architect Zaha Hadid would be noteworthy enough simply for her prominence as a woman in a male-dominated field. But her striking and uncompromising buildings, which showcase her affection for dramatic slopes, angles and undulations, have made Hadid a favorite among art galleries and clothing designers looking to make a statement. Hadid, 62, has been delighting her fellow "starchitects" for years—she won the Pritzker Prize in 2004 and was named to the TIME 100 list in 2010—but in 2012 she turned the eyes of a wider audience with a pair of dazzling buildings: the Aquatics Centre for the London Olympics and the Heydar Aliyev Cultural Center in Azerbaijan *(see page 94)*. The ever stylish Hadid told TIME, "There is a connection between architecture and fashion because of the way the body is placed within that space."

# Nation

FROM LEFT: TOM PENNINGTON—GETTY IMAGES; YANG LEI—XINHUA
PRESS/CORBIS; CHRIS MADDALONI—CQ ROLL CALL/GETTY IMAGES

VISIONS OF AMERICA

*Left: U.S. Navy veteran Stephen E. Sherman, 91, was the oldest delegate to attend the Democratic National Convention in Charlotte, N.C., in September.*

*Center: A woman places flowers at a makeshift memorial for victims of a mass shooting in Aurora, Colo.*

*Right: Demonstrators rally to support the Affordable Care Act outside the U.S. Supreme Court building on June 28.*

# Four More Years: Obama Prevails

The President defeats challenger Mitt Romney in an election that winds up settling very little

A subtle message about things to come may have been planted in the victory speech. The re-elected President, having proved that he can win by brawling and not just by floating on gossamer dreams, announced a new era of mature discipline—starting at home. Four years ago, Barack

Obama delivered hope and change to his daughters in the lovable form of a brand-new puppy. This time around, all they got was a pat on the head. "Sasha and Malia," he said before an adoring—and relieved—crowd in Chicago's Mc-Cormick Place, "I'm so proud of you guys. But I will say that for now, one dog's probably enough."

It was a fitting end to a one-dog's-enough sort of campaign. For months, even years, the President and the challenger postured, attacked, dodged and debated. They and their supporters begged and spent crazy money—not millions but billions—yet somehow, fairly or unfairly, both candidates wound up looking a bit undersized. Obama once stirred multitudes in a football stadium against a backdrop of Greek pillars. Now he is mortal again, hav-

ing earned roughly 9 million fewer votes than he won in 2008. A very crafty, very skilled mortal, politically speaking: Obama figured out how to leverage a thumping victory from relative weakness.

Republican Mitt Romney, who once saved the Olympics in Salt Lake City and traded companies the way children trade Pokémon cards, worked for five years and leveraged nothing. By clawing back the GOP bastions of Indiana and North Carolina, he managed to cut Obama's electoral-vote margin by 26 from the last time out, yet he lost one battleground after another, his campaign exhausted on such molehills as who should pay for Big Bird.

Obama became the first re-elected President in more than a century whose share of the vote was smaller his

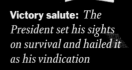

**Victory salute:** *The President set his sights on survival and hailed it as his vindication*

CHIP SOMODEV___—GETTY IMAGES

**Self-sabotage:** *A defeated Romney often seemed to be the Obama campaign's wordsmith, keeping his foes stocked with zingers*

second time around. With a sluggish economy tugging at him like an anchor and a single-minded opposition dedicated to drowning him, the President set his sights on mere survival and welcomed it as his vindication. After all, in these harrowing times of stalled economies and cultural upheaval, survival is the new winning. Today's answer to "How are you doing?" is "Compared with what?" One dog, in other words, is enough.

Once billed as a decisive moment in American history, the long and sour election wound up settling very little. Leadership in Washington remained unchanged: Obama in the White House, Democrat Harry Reid in the Senate, Republican John Boehner in the House. Some $6 billion of campaign spending delivered another near tie to what has become a fifty-fifty America. In fact, the election results undercut one of the few points of political agreement among Americans in recent years. Most people believe that Washington is broken, or so they tell pollsters. Some blame the President and his fellow Democrats, with their vigorous agenda of deficit spending, health care for all and a green industrial policy. Some blame the naysaying Republicans, who have resisted Obama each step of the way and were rewarded with a midterm surge in 2010. But nearly every survey found a deep desire among the public for something different from the Federal Government.

Come Election Day, those wishes effectively canceled each other out. Nearly 120 million voters cast their ballots, and the net effect was no change at all. America went shopping for a new car and returned home with the same coughing jalopy. You have to dig deeply into the balloting to find anyone voted off the Washington island. A paltry handful of seats switched in the House of Representatives, while Republicans kicked away another chance to take control of the Senate by nominating extreme candidates who used their soapboxes, in a few decisive cases, to air their peculiar views on the theology and biology of sexual assault.

As the saying goes in Silicon Valley, this result was not a bug in the software; it was a feature of it—the unsurprising result of carefully hatched plans at party headquarters in Chicago and Boston. Both sides put their fingers in the political winds many months ago, decided that the public would split evenly and built their strategies around that certainty. Expecting a close election, they focused their energies on stirring up their core supporters while stinting on vision and stoking fear. They flooded the ether with negative ads and steered clear of fresh ideas as if they were cow pies. So instead of a campaign about the future of the country, it was, by mutual agreement of the political-consulting industry, a campaign about turnout in a relative handful of battleground counties.

Ultimately, Obama was buoyed by a segment of the

CHARLES DHARAPAK—AP

**Dustup** *Obama seemed lethargic in the first debate, but the two contenders tangled in the second debate, on Long Island, N.Y., above, where the candidates grew testy*

electorate he was never supposed to win: the forgotten white men he once dismissed as "bitter" and clinging "to guns or religion or antipathy to people who are not like them." Obama retained just enough of them in his coalition of liberals, young people, working women, African Americans and Latinos. The result was a string of wins in the industrial Midwest that slammed the door on any possible Romney path to victory. For many months these Rust Belt, lunch-bucket voters had been fed a steady diet of well-tailored messages that boiled down to this: sharp guys wearing soft suits and perfect haircuts have been shutting your factories and offshoring your jobs for decades, and now get a load of Mitt Romney. The fact that Romney had opposed Obama's bailout of General Motors and Chrysler—giants of an industry that employs, directly or indirectly, hundreds of thousands of workers in Ohio and nearby states—more than sealed the deal. Between Romney's position on the government rescue of Detroit and his party's bristling line on Latino immigration, Obama had what he needed to build his firewalls.

The survivor took the stage well after midnight, having waited more than 90 minutes for the concession call

## ELECTION BY THE NUMBERS

**20** *The number of debates conducted by Republican candidates over the course of 2011-12 as they vied for their party's nomination*

**$661 million**
*Amount of money raised by the 1,063 super PACs registered to participate in the 2012 campaign*

**294** *Number of campaign stops made by Mitt Romney over the course of the campaign. President Obama made 227 stops*

**237** *Estimated number of the 435 House seats in the new Congress that will be held by Republicans. Democrats could hold 189. Nine seats were undecided at press time*

from a stunned Romney. Four years earlier, at Grant Park in Chicago, the young Illinois Senator described his decisive win as a mandate for change—only to find that victory speeches expire in Washington quicker than the warranty on a bootleg wristwatch. Each bold step President Obama took toward his sweeping agenda brought him a little deeper into the mud, until he was swamped in the wake of the Tea Party speedboat. Four years later, the struggle was visible in each gray hair on his head.

"I know that political campaigns can sometimes seem small, even silly," Obama said. But politics "is important," not least in a campaign like this one. "Democracy in a nation of 300 million can be noisy and messy and complicated," he continued. "We have our own opinions. Each of us has deeply held beliefs. And when we go through tough times, when we make big decisions as a country, it necessarily stirs passions, stirs up controversy ... These arguments we have are a mark of our liberty."

**Two Spent Forces** Obama made no promises of bold new programs. Instead he pledged to work on cutting the deficit, overhauling the tax code and bridging the divide on immigration. Any trouble he has in claiming a larger mandate for a second term is in part because he never really sought one. It's easy to forget that 2012 was a new experience for him, the first time Obama faced a vigorous re-election challenge—for any office. His political career until now had almost always been a one-way escalator gliding up, up, up. His swoon in the polls a month before the voting was his first encounter with the law of gravity, and he got quite close to earth before his chute opened.

If his first presidential campaign could be distilled into a single moment, it might be the day in July 2008 when he was visiting U.S. troops in Kuwait, was handed a basketball in a gymnasium—then launched a three-pointer that carved a rainbow on its way to the pot of gold. His 53% share of the popular vote four months later was the largest any Democrat had won in more than 40 years.

This time around, Obama's game plan involved trad-

MIKE SEGAR—REUTERS

## Paul Ryan: Looking Ahead

He was just 28 when he entered the House in 1999. The budget was balanced. The stock market was booming. But Paul Ryan, child of a blue-collar district in Wisconsin and a disciple of the theories of Ayn Rand, was fixated on the impossible arithmetic of the U.S.'s long-term fiscal commitments. So he worked his way up the Budget Committee ladder, following advice he was given by the liberal Barney Frank of Massachusetts: The way to have an impact in Congress is to "be a specialist, not a generalist."

Frank's advice has served Ryan well, and never more so than when Ryan floated a proposed budget overhaul in 2010 that caught the fancy of the emerging Tea Party by calling for major changes in the government's social safety net in order to address its long-term fiscal woes. The bold proposals outraged Democrats but quickly made Ryan one of the leaders of the national debate on federal budgetary policy, and fiscal-hawk Republicans were delighted when Mitt Romney announced on Aug. 11 that Ryan would be Romney's running mate in the 2012 presidential campaign.

A committed and devoutly pro-life Roman Catholic, Ryan, 42, is an ardent outdoorsman, hunter and fitness buff who was voted "the Hill's No. 1 gym rat" by congressional staffers. Despite his ticket's loss in the campaign, he gained wide national attention and will be at the heart of the negotiations that will shape the future of budgetary policy from his powerful post as chairman of the Budget Committee.

ing elbows beneath the basket. With the public not sold on his signature first-term achievement—the mammoth enterprise known as Obamacare—he and his allies decided to go negative early, pouring hundreds of millions of dollars into a summertime ad blitz targeted at swing-state voters. The idea was to paint Romney in lurid colors as Scrooge McDuck minus the spats, a Bain plutocrat who swam in gold coins that he looted from once proud companies before firing their hardworking employees.

It was a page ripped from the GOP's soiled 2004 playbook. In that year, President George W. Bush overcame his weakness in the polls by savaging his challenger, John Kerry of Massachusetts. Romney fought back with tactics similar to Obama's, though various spending rules meant that his negative barrage started later. By the final days of campaigning, according to one analysis, nearly 90% of campaign ads in the battleground states were negative.

Yet Romney often seemed to be the Obama campaign's unpaid wordsmith, keeping the re-election campaign

### This is the system we have, and it has proved durable and strong. But that doesn't make it pretty

stocked with zingers—the most lethal of which was from his speech to a group of high-rollers on the topic of Americans who don't pay federal income tax. The "47%," as he called this near majority, believe they are "victims" and constitute a drag on society. The remark surely hurt him with the millions of retirees, troops, students and low-paid workers who rightly feel like contributing citizens.

The incumbent opened a lead in September, after the party conventions. In Charlotte, N.C., former President Bill Clinton gave a bravura defense of his wife's onetime rival. It was perhaps the first speech of the campaign with any resonance, and the last. But then Obama and Romney made their first side-by-side appearance in a debate at the University of Denver on Oct. 3. Romney did not look nearly as frightening as the President's ads suggested. Obama, however, with his low-energy performance, appeared to be every bit the spent force that Romney's negative script depicted. By a Gallup Poll–record 52-point margin, the viewing public crowned Romney the winner.

It seems that Obama, in a burst of overconfidence, had canceled many of his prep sessions and had got it into his head that he didn't need to engage the earnest Romney while millions watched. The post-Denver polls showed a whole new race, one suddenly too close to call. By some

STEVE HELBER—AP

measures, the contest entered the final 10 days with public opinion almost exactly where it was in midsummer: all that heat and noise, and nothing had happened.

And then the ancient forecast of an October surprise came true, right on schedule, when a storm named Sandy doused the lights and distracted the country. Having learned well the lessons of Katrina, Obama tore up his travel schedule to keep watch from the White House as Sandy shoved a wall of water into the North Atlantic coastline. The storm diverted attention in the New York–based media and left Romney with little to do but bag relief donations and keep his lip zipped. In Boston, Romney staffers seethed as New Jersey Governor Chris Christie, the keynote speaker at the GOP Convention, praised

Obama's quick response and toured the ruins with the President by his side. According to some exit polls, voters likewise approved of Obama's storm performance, giving him the boost he needed to seal his win.

Obama's re-election and the continued split in Congress confirmed a reality that has been forming for a generation: no matter how passionately the true believers in each party make their case, no matter what new technologies arrive to amplify their voices, no matter how high the Alps of campaign cash lavished on data mining, hyper-targeted ads and voter mobilization become, Americans refuse to give a governing mandate to one side or the other. The U.S. is—for the moment, at least—a two-party system with no-party rule. Since 1984, seven presidential

## Conventions, Hurricane Isaac and Other Hot-Air Masses
Republicans convene in Tampa, Fla., to nominate Mitt Romney, where a big storm intrudes. Democrats gather in Charlotte, N.C., and Bill Clinton steals the show

Republican delegates arrived in Tampa for their national convention eager to rally around their candidate, Mitt Romney. But the first night's events had to be called off due to an uninvited visitor, Hurricane Isaac. When the convention came

to order on Aug. 28, a parade of Hispanic, black and youthful speakers took the stage—although many commentators noted that the delegates were primarily older, white Americans. The respected GOP Senator Lindsey Graham of South Carolina bluntly warned his colleagues, "We're not generating enough angry white guys to stay in business for the long term."

The gathering's standout speakers included New Jersey Governor Chris Christie, who delivered the keynote speech; Florida Senator Marco Rubio, a rising star in the GOP; and a smart, funny Ann Romney, above. After an off-key introduction by movie legend Clint Eastwood, Romney roused his audience with an upbeat call to "restore the promise of America."

Democrats convened in Charlotte on Sept. 3 feeling upbeat about their chances for a November victory. Indeed, TIME political analyst Joe Klein noted "a slightly smug lassitude affecting the Democrats, convinced as they are of their own rectitude and the extremist depredations of the GOP." Klein's advice to the Democrats as they move forward: Abandon your emphasis on identity politics and seek to widen your appeal to mainstream white Americans.

A pack of stellar speakers got the party faithful cheering, including a rousing Michelle Obama and a tough-talking Joe Biden. The President's acceptance speech was eloquent and well received, but was no barn-burner. Indeed, the undisputed star of the Democrats' show was former President Bill Clinton, whose rambling but incisive attack on GOP policies led the President to joke that Clinton should be named "Secretary of Explaining Stuff."

LEFT: SCOTT EELLS—BLOOMBERG/GETTY IMAGES; RIGHT: DANIEL ACKER—BLOOMBERG/GETTY IMAGES

## Forward Steps for Same-Sex Marriage and Legalized Pot

On election night, two evolving social issues commanded wide attention. Voters in Colorado, Washington and Oregon had the opportunity to make history by voting on initiatives that would legalize recreational use and sales of marijuana in their respective states. Only residents of Oregon rejected the move. Massachusetts voters also joined the 17 states and the District of Columbia that allow medical use of the drug.

Washington State's law calls for a licensing regimen for growers and sellers. It bans sales to people under 21 and sets a 25% tax on sales, which will fund drug-abuse prevention, schools and health insurance. It sets a legal limit on blood levels of THC, pot's active ingredient, for driving. The law bans growing for personal use.

Colorado's new law, which supporters are toasting above, allows personal possession and growing for one's own use or to give away. Sales, however, will require a license and will be taxed to fund school construction, at a rate of up to 15%. Both measures may result in clashes with the Federal Government, which continues to outlaw marijuana as illegal.

In a sign that social acceptance of same-sex marriage is rapidly increasing, Maine and Maryland voted to legalize gay marriage, each by about 5%. Washington State's proposal passed by 4%, and Minnesota voted down a ban on same-sex marriage.

elections have gone by without a popular-vote landslide of 55% or more. That hasn't happened since the late 19th century. Political scientists keep writing books saying a robust majority is on its way, to be gathered by one party or the other. Once again, though, the emerging majority failed to emerge. We're still waiting.

**Will the Fever Be Unbroken?** If they are honest with themselves, Republicans will recognize in defeat that the party made Romney's job more rather than less difficult. Beginning with the almost comical anybody-but-Romney spectacle of the GOP primaries, where a parade of has-beens, not-yets and never-weres competed to flank Romney on the right, the party coaxed and prodded its candidate into damaging positions on immigration, abortion, gay rights and more. A party interested in winning future presidential elections would ask itself why candidates who might have been more adept campaigners than Romney chose to stay on the sidelines this year. And why did Romney's poll numbers jump only after the Denver debate, in which he reassured voters that he would be a moderate, open-minded President? There was a message for the right wing in that surge. But there are powerful interests in the party—from evangelical preachers to talk-show hotheads to leaders of right-wing pressure groups—who are more interested in ideological orthodoxy than in winning elections.

As for the President and the Democrats, they took their eye off the ball—the economy—too early, passing

LEFT: BRENNAN LINSLEY—AP. CENTER: JIM LO SCALZO—EPA

**Morning in America** *Voters line up to cast their ballots as dawn breaks at Nottoway Park in Vienna, Va.*

TOP ROW, FROM LEFT: MIKE RANSDELL—AP; REX FEATURES—AP; CENTER: ELISE AMENDOLA—AP (2). BOTTOM: GARY PORTER—MILWAUKEE JOURNAL SENTINEL/AP; MORRY GASH—AP

the hugely ambitious Affordable Care Act on a party-line vote. Obama is unlikely to make the same mistake again. The signature accomplishment of his second term, if he can pull it off, will be not an expansion of entitlements but a reduction of them. He will sooner or later reach for the Grand Compromise that has eluded Washington for nearly 30 years: trading lower taxes on businesses and individuals for closing billions in loopholes and other tax-code giveaways that make virtually everyone in the U.S.—from corporations to small businesses to college students—welfare queens of one kind or another.

The question always comes up after a presidential campaign, but especially in tough times: Who would want this job? And so it is worth remembering, always, that credit goes to the men and women who are willing to put themselves on the line, because it is often unpleasant and never easy but always vitally important. Barack Hussein Obama and Willard ("Mitt") Romney stepped up to the fight this year; they campaigned doggedly (if not always well) and opened themselves to withering attacks not only on their political positions but also on their morals and good faith. This is the system we have, and it has proved durable and strong. But that doesn't make it pretty. In the end, each gave as good as he got, and Obama squeaked through. Ordeal? Yes. Uplift? Alas, no. ∎

—*By David Von Drehle*

## A Congress Still Divided

**R**epublicans entertained high hopes of winning a majority in the Senate, but blunders by weak candidates ended up adding to the Democratic majority, which will now be 54-45, with one independent who leans Democrat. Republicans kept their firm grasp of the House, but they will now enjoy a smaller majority. Below, three surprising Senate races:

### Missouri

■ **Todd Akin** *The strongly pro-life House member torpedoed his chances with his remarks on "legitimate rape"*

■ **Claire McCaskill** *Considered the Senate's most vulnerable Democrat, McCaskill rode Akin's gaffe to a commanding victory*

### Massachusetts

■ **Scott Brown** *The likable moderate who won Ted Kennedy's old seat in 2010 was leading until Warren found her stride*

■ **Elizabeth Warren** *The Harvard professor stumbled early in the race, but quickly improved to beat Brown in an upset*

### Wisconsin

■ **Tommy Thompson** *The state's popular former governor, now 70, was successfully labeled out of touch by opponent Baldwin*

■ **Tammy Baldwin** *The seven-term Congresswoman won in a major upset and will be the nation's first openly gay Senator*

**Analyzed** *In battleground state Ohio, the data-mining operation profiled 29,000 voters—and gave some of them incentives to act*

# Delving for Votes

## The Obama campaign's secret weapon: mastery of data

LATE IN THE SPRING OF 2012, THE BACKROOM number crunchers who powered Barack Obama's campaign to victory noticed that George Clooney had an almost gravitational tug on West Coast females ages 40 to 49. The women were far and away the single demographic group most likely to hand over cash, for a chance to dine in Hollywood with Clooney—and Obama. So as they did with all the other data collected, stored and analyzed in the two-year drive for re-election, Obama's top campaign aides decided to put this insight to use. They sought out an East Coast celebrity who had similar appeal among the same demographic, aiming to replicate the millions of dollars produced by the Clooney contest. "We were blessed with an overflowing menu of options, but we chose Sarah Jessica Parker," explains a senior campaign adviser. And so the next Dinner with Barack contest was born: a chance to eat at Parker's West Village brownstone in Manhattan.

For the general public, there was no way to know that the idea for the Parker contest had come from a data-mining discovery about some Obama supporters: affection for contests, small dinners and celebrity. But from the beginning, campaign manager Jim Messina had promised a totally different, metric-driven kind of campaign in which politics was the goal but political instincts might not be the means. "We are going to measure every single thing in this campaign," he said after taking the job. He proceeded to hire an analytics department five times as large as that of the 2008 operation.

Exactly what that team of dozens of data crunchers was doing, however, was a closely held secret. "They are our nuclear codes," campaign spokesman Ben LaBolt said when asked about their algorithms. Around the office, data-mining experiments were given mysterious code names such as Narwhal and Dreamcatcher. The team even worked at a remove from the rest of the campaign staff, setting up shop in a windowless room at the vast headquarters office in Chicago. The "scientists" created

LEFT: EVAN VUCCI—AP; RIGHT: DANIEL SHEA

regular briefings on their work for the President and top aides, but public details were in short supply as the campaign guarded what it believed to be its biggest institutional advantage over Mitt Romney's campaign: its data.

On Nov. 4, a group of senior campaign advisers agreed to describe their cutting-edge efforts with TIME, to be published only after the winner was declared. What they revealed as they pulled back the curtain was a massive data effort that helped Obama raise $1 billion, remade the process of targeting TV ads and created detailed models of swing-state voters that could be used to increase the effectiveness of everything from phone calls and door knocks to direct mailings and social media.

The new approach also allowed the campaign to raise more money than it had once thought possible. A large portion of the cash raised online came through an intricate, metric-driven e-mail campaign in which dozens of fund-raising appeals went out each day. Many of these e-mails were just tests, with different subject lines, senders and messages. Inside the campaign, there were office pools on which combination would raise the most money, and often the results were a surprise. Michelle Obama's e-mails performed best early on, and at times, campaign boss Messina's performed better than Vice President Joe Biden's. In many cases, the top performers raised 10 times as much money for the campaign as the underperformers.

Chicago discovered that people who signed up for the campaign's Quick Donate program, which allowed repeat giving online or via text message without having to re-enter credit-card information, gave about four times as much as other donors. So the program was expanded and incentivized. By the end of October, Quick Donate had become a big part of the campaign's messaging to supporters, and first-time donors were offered a free bumper sticker to sign up.

The magic tricks that opened wallets were then repurposed to turn out votes. The analytics team used four streams of polling data to build a detailed picture of voters in key states. In the last weeks of the campaign, said one official, the analytics team had polling data from about 29,000 people in Ohio alone—a whopping sample that composed nearly half of 1% of all voters there—allowing for deep dives into exactly where each demographic and regional group was trending at any given moment. This was a huge advantage: when polls started to slip after the first debate, the campaign could check to see which voters were changing sides and which were not.

It was this database that helped steady campaign aides in October's choppy waters, assuring them that most of the Ohioans in motion were not Obama backers but likely Romney supporters whom Romney had lost because of his September blunders. Online, the get-out-the-vote effort continued with a first-ever attempt at using Facebook on a mass scale to replicate the door-knocking efforts of field organizers. Late in the campaign, people who had downloaded an app were sent messages with pictures of their friends in swing states. They were told to click a button to automatically urge those targeted voters to register to vote, vote early or help others get to the polls. The campaign found that roughly 1 in 5 people contacted by a Facebook pal acted on the request, in large part because the message came from someone they knew.

Data helped drive the campaign's ad buying too. Rather than relying on outside media consultants to decide where ads should run, Messina based his purchases on the massive internal data sets. "We were able to put our target voters through some really complicated modeling, to say, O.K., if Miami-Dade women under 35 are the targets, [here is] how to reach them," said one official. As a result, the campaign bought ads to air during unconventional programming, like *Sons of Anarchy* and *The Walking Dead*, skirting the traditional route of buying ads next to local news programming. That data-driven decision-making played a huge role in creating a second term for the 44th President and will be one of the more closely studied elements of the 2012 cycle. It's another sign that the role of the campaign pros in Washington who make decisions on hunches and experience is rapidly dwindling, being replaced by the work of quants and computer aces who can crack massive data sets for insight. As one Obama staffer put it, the time of "guys sitting in a back room smoking cigars, saying 'We always buy *60 Minutes*'" is over. In politics, the era of big data has arrived. ■

—*By Michael Scherer*

**Beep!** *Inside the Obama campaign's computer analysis "cave," number crunchers employ data mining as a political tool*

# Superstorm!

# The East Coast Is Devastated When Sandy Surges Ashore

O N OCT. 29, 2012, SUPERSTORM SANDY PICKED up the Atlantic Ocean and hurled it at the U.S. Northeast coast, driving before it a storm surge that inundated vast sections of New York City and obliterated the New Jersey shoreline for hundreds of miles, from Atlantic City to Philadelphia. Across 21 states, from North Carolina to Maine and as far west as Michigan, the massive storm left more than 100 people dead and some 8.5 million without power, and it likely caused more than $20 billion in damages.

Sandy, which sprang to life as a trough of low-pressure air in the Caribbean on Oct. 19, had become a major catastrophe and one of the worst natural disasters ever to strike the U.S. Watching in horror, Americans wondered why the storm was so devastating, how long it would take the region and the nation to recover, and how Americans could prepare for similar weather disasters in the future.

**Storm warnings.** To understand Sandy, start with this fact: it was a monster. Rather than a single storm, Sandy was a hybrid, a "Frankenstorm." Formed in the western Caribbean Sea, the tropical cyclone moved east, pounding Cuba and Haiti and claiming 71 lives. Then it moved north, drawing energy from the sharp differences in temperature and air pressure coming from an atmospheric blocking pattern in the North Atlantic. A storm like Sandy usually veers off harmlessly into the Atlantic when it strikes in the autumn, but that Arctic air pattern forced Sandy to take a hard left and slam directly into the heavily populated Northeast as a superstorm, a freak of rare chance, Mother Nature's power on steroids.

The result was a mammoth storm that battered coasts, towns and cities across one-third of the U.S., stretching from the Carolinas to Maine and from Long Island to Chicago and the Great Lakes. With its winds measuring some 1,000 miles (1,609 km) in diameter, Sandy covered more territory than any storm to hit the U.S.—ever.

Sandy was more than a monster: it was also a shape-shifter. In the Carolinas and along the Jersey Shore, its pounding waves obliterated shorelines, devastated beach

**Battered** *The storm surge and fires devastated Mantoloking, N.J., an upscale community on the Barnegat Peninsula*

DOUG MILLS—THE NEW YORK TIMES/REDUX

houses and inundated the streets of resort towns. Erasing legends, Sandy tore up portions of the Atlantic City boardwalk, ruined Victorian-era houses in Cape May, N.J., and destroyed the fishing pier in Ocean City, Md.

In leafy suburbs in Pennsylvania, New York State and New England, Sandy's wrath was felt most powerfully as sustained winds that reached 80 m.p.h., downing power lines and toppling trees that killed people who took shelter inside houses below. In New York City, Sandy's power to devastate was felt in the potent surge the storm's winds pushed ahead of it. In Battery Park in lower Manhattan, the surge topped out at 13.88 ft. (4.2 m), far surpassing predictions and previous records, as waters rushed over seawalls and left vast swaths of the area underwater.

In the upper Midwest, Sandy took the form of high winds that whipped up huge waves on the Great Lakes, halting shipping. In its most freakish manifestation, Sandy dumped a rare late-October blizzard on the Appalachians that measured 28 in. (71 cm) in Redhouse, Md.

**The storm's price.** If Sandy was a monster and a shapeshifter, it was also a killer: as of Nov. 5, more than 100 deaths had been attributed to the storm. But in most of the areas affected by its rains, winds and storm surges,

## SANDY BY THE NUMBERS

# 48 Hours

*Number of hours that Sandy shut down trading on the New York Stock Exchange, the market's longest hiatus due to weather since the great blizzard of 1888*

# 21

*Number of states directly affected by the superstorm, ranging from states on the East Coast to Maine in the north and Illinois in the Midwest*

# 8.5 million

*Number of Americans left without power by the storm as its peak impact was felt in the morning hours of Tuesday, Oct. 30, representing 7% of the population*

**Onslaught** *At far left, rescue personnel assist Haley Rombi, 3, on Staten Island on Oct. 30.*
*This page, clockwise from left: floodwaters pour down a parking garage ramp in the Financial District in New York City.*
*Floodwaters rush into a PATH commuter rail station connecting Manhattan to Hoboken, N.J.*
*A construction crane at a high-end apartment building collapses in Manhattan.*

LEFT PAGE: MICHAEL KIRBY SMITH/THE NEW YORK TIMES/REDUX. RIGHT PAGE, CLOCKWISE FROM LEFT: ANDREW BURTON/GETTY IMAGES; PORT AUTHORITY OF NY AND NJ/AP; ALLISON JOYCE/GETTY IMAGES

Sandy's effects were not measured in death tolls. More a mugger or vandal than a killer, the big storm confined hundreds of thousands of people in their homes with no power, and left tens of thousands of others homeless.

Sandy paralyzed New York City, shutting down its public schools, its streets and its three major airports. In a city that functions only because millions of people commute to Manhattan Island every day via mass transit, Sandy halted service on commuter rail lines and shut down auto, subway and train tunnels that run beneath the Hudson and East rivers. Floodwaters coursed through some subway tunnels; the entire system was shut down for three days, and officials warned it would be weeks before full normal service would resume.

In a cutoff Manhattan Island, geography became destiny. The lights remained on in most neighborhoods, but when an explosion ripped through a downtown Con Edison substation at 8:30 p.m. on Oct. 29, the lower third of Manhattan went dark, trapping thousands of people without elevator service in high-rise apartment buildings.

In Breezy Point, a Queens beachfront community, high winds sent a fire whipping through the neighborhood. Frustrated fire fighters, some of whom lived in the tight-knit, largely Irish-American community, could only watch in frustration as the storm surge made streets impassable and covered water hydrants. By the time the flames were put out, 111 homes had burned down.

**Fighting back.** Damaging as Sandy was, it might have wreaked further havoc if federal, state and local officials had not worked strenuously before the storm made landfall to mitigate its effects. Authorities convinced many citizens to evacuate low-lying sections of major cities and imperiled seaside towns. Governors Chris Christie of New Jersey and Andrew Cuomo of New York, along with Mayor Michael Bloomberg of New York City, offered calm, measured guidance before, during and after the storm, and their efforts were widely hailed as models for other public servants to follow in future calamities.

The storm not only shut down the East Coast; it also put the brakes on the hard-fought presidential election only

## "Anything that I've asked for, he's gotten to me ... He's done a great job for New Jersey."

—GOVERNOR CHRIS CHRISTIE, ON PRESIDENT OBAMA

31

**Aftermath** *This page, clockwise from left: President Obama and Governor Christie visit with evacuees at a community center in Brigantine, N.J.*

*Hoboken, N.J., residents use shopping bags for protection as they walk through sewage-polluted waters.*

*A woman surveys the ruins of Breezy Point, N.Y., after fires burned down 111 homes in the area.*

*Far right: State Highway 12 in North Carolina's Outer Banks buckled under Sandy's storm surge.*

a week before voters were due to cast their ballots. Both President Barack Obama and challenger Mitt Romney suspended campaigning. Early on, Obama supervised the federal response from the White House, winning a surprising endorsement from Christie, a Republican, who said, "He's been very attentive, and anything that I've asked for, he's gotten to me … He's done a great job for New Jersey." Romney turned a planned campaign rally in Ohio into a "relief event," but there was little he could do to match Obama's direct engagement with the disaster.

On Wednesday, Oct. 31, Obama joined Christie in touring devastated areas of New Jersey and visiting with storm victims. The odd-couple pairing offered good fodder for Beltway pundits to chew on, but Christie, an outspoken foe of the President in the past, had a sharp retort for his critics: "I've got a job to do here in New Jersey that's much bigger than presidential politics, and I could care less about any of that stuff."

New York City struggled to return to normal on Oct. 31, but gridlock reigned as commuters turned to autos to reach Manhattan; officials mandated that only vehicles carrying at least three people could cross bridges to enter the city. Airports resumed some service by week's end, as did commuter rail lines and limited subway service.

New Jersey had borne the brunt of Sandy's power,

and the Garden State's recovery efforts promised to be long and vexing. In Hoboken, Newark and Atlantic City, streets were filled with water, oil and raw sewage days after the storm, power remained out, and National Guard troops were still rescuing survivors trapped in apartment buildings and homes. By the first weekend after the storm, patience was running out—as was the region's vital supply of gas—and a vast social crisis was looming, even as colder weather was arriving. And all along the Atlantic Coast, homeowners and proprietors of restaurants, amusement parks and motels were forced to confront a hard question: not simply how to rebuild but, as big storms become more frequent, whether or not to rebuild.

**Looking ahead.** If Sandy achieved one positive outcome, it was to force Americans to confront the future. As TIME environment correspondent Bryan Walsh pointed out, "Thanks to a combination of factors—more people and property in vulnerable coastal areas as well as climate change—we're likely to experience disasters on the scale of Sandy more often in the future." Walsh offered five proposals for citizens and public officials to ponder. First: Make sure you can see ahead—which includes updating the nation's aging system of weather-monitoring satellites. Second: Build a better grid to replace America's

LEFT PAGE, CLOCKWISE FROM LEFT: DOUG MILLS—THE NEW YORK TIMES/REDUX; RICHARD PERRY/THE NEW YORK TIMES/REDUX; SPENCER PLATT—GETTY IMAGES. RIGHT PAGE: STEVE EARLEY—THE VIRGINIAN-PILOT/AP

## SANDY BY THE NUMBERS

# $20 billion

*Estimate of total damages Sandy may create, offered by Charles Watson, an executive at hazard-research firm Kinetic Analysis Corp. in Silver Spring, Md. Other estimates ranged as high as $50 billion*

# 25

*Percentage of the nation's cell sites put out of service on Oct. 30 by Sandy, according to FCC Chairman Julius Genachowski*

# 16,000

*Number of airline flights cancelled in the U.S. due to Sandy. Analysts estimated some 50,000 airline travelers had their plans affected by the storm*

creaky but essential electrical infrastructure. Third: Realize we are all in this together. Normally in a disaster, the hardest-hit states can borrow emergency personnel or utility crews from unscathed neighbors under mutual-aid agreements. Sandy's size made that virtually impossible.

Walsh's fourth suggestion: Stop ignoring the climate connection. Climate change has caused sea levels to rise, which made Sandy's storm surges and coastal flooding all the more devastating. Overall sea levels have risen by 8 in. (20 cm) in recent years, and the rate has been accelerating recently. That puts coastal cities like Washington, New Orleans and Miami at growing risk for major floods every time a storm strikes.

Finally, Walsh proposed: Prepare for the worst. Today, more than 150 million Americans live in coastal counties, and at least 3.5 million live within a few feet of high tide. So when a storm like Sandy strikes, more people and property are in harm's way. Besides cutting carbon emissions, we'll need to adapt to the effects of climate change by building infrastructure that can withstand the devastating coastal storm surges that will become only more common as sea levels rise because of warming. If Sandy was a monster, a shape-shifter and a mugger, perhaps the storm could also be a teacher, reminding us that if we don't pay now, we'll certainly pay more dearly later. ∎

# Supreme Surprise

Chief Justice John Roberts casts an unexpected deciding vote as the Supreme Court rules on the Affordable Care Act

YOU DON'T HAVE TO LOVE CLASSICAL MUSIC to be amazed that Beethoven wrote his *Ninth Symphony* while deaf, or be a fan of the old New York Giants to marvel at Willie Mays' catch in Game 1 of the 1954 World Series. For legal buffs, the virtuoso performance of Chief Justice John Roberts in deciding the biggest case of his career to date was just that sort of jaw dropper, no matter how they might feel about the Patient Protection and Affordable Care Act, a.k.a. Obamacare, the landmark 2010 health-care-reform law that includes a controversial individual mandate that will require most Americans to purchase insurance.

Not since King Solomon offered to split the baby has a judge engineered a slicker solution to a bitterly divisive dispute. With his fellow Supreme Court Justices split 4 to 4 between two extreme outcomes—blessing the sprawling law or killing it—Roberts maneuvered half the court into signing part of his ruling and the other half into endorsing the rest. He gave the liberals their long-cherished dream of government-led reform while giving his fellow conservatives a new avenue to limit congressional power, which they have been seeking since the New Deal.

With the court's approval ratings at record lows and supporters of President Barack Obama grimly predicting a legal travesty—or even a judicial coup—Roberts somehow cloaked a win for right-leaning legal theory in the glittering garb of a triumph for the left. And the Democratic swords that were being sharpened for an election-year war against the court were hammered into trumpets with which to herald the statesmanship of the Republican

Sotomayor
YES

Breyer
YES

Alito
NO

Kagan
YES

Thomas
NO

Scalia
NO

Roberts
YES

Kennedy
NO

Ginsburg
YES

**The fact that Roberts had to squirm like Houdini to reach middle ground only enhanced the bravura of the feat**

LEFT: EVAN GOLUB—DEMOTIX/CORBIS; RIGHT: PABLO MARINEX MONSIVAIS—AP PHOTO

**Class picture** *Above, the nine Justices posed for a portrait in 2010; each Justice's vote on the 2012 Obamacare decision is noted. At left, foes of the Affordable Care Act rally outside the Supreme Court on June 28; supporters also demonstrated*

Chief Justice. "Whatever the politics, today's decision was a victory for people all over this country," the President declared after the June 28 ruling. Sharp-eyed conservative commentators—George Will and Charles Krauthammer, for example—read the fine print and agreed, though for very different reasons.

Many on the right, however, refused to see a silver lining in this defeat snatched from the jaws of victory. "The particular tragedy is that four Justices would have overturned … all of Obamacare as unconstitutional," the *Wall Street Journal* editorial board lamented. "Only John Roberts prevented it."

The fact that Roberts had to squirm like Houdini to reach middle ground (in the second part of his ruling, he held that the mandate to buy insurance is not a tax, but by the third section he announced that it is) only enhanced the bravura of the feat. Philosophical purity is easy—the blogosphere is lousy with it—while pragmatic solutions to difficult problems are as rare these days as virgins on *Jersey Shore*. As such, the Chief Justice's ruling confounded a political world primed for Armageddon: the spectacle of five Republican appointees striking down the signature achievement of a Democratic President in the midst of a tough re-election campaign. After a party-line vote by the court to decide the disputed 2000 election for George W.

Bush over Al Gore, and another in the controversial 2010 *Citizens United* campaign-spending case, the Washington atmosphere reeked of gasoline, and the Obamacare case looked like a match ready to drop.

By setting a limit on congressional power to regulate the nation's commerce and by ruling that Congress cannot use its spending power to force states to greatly expand Medicaid coverage, Roberts blazed legal trails that conservatives have long dreamed of. How far down those paths the court will go in future terms is anyone's guess, but the liberal Justice Ruth Bader Ginsburg was sufficiently worried about these precedents that she wrote a lengthy dissent, even though she had gotten the end result she wanted: Obamacare was upheld. And her three liberal colleagues substantially agreed with her.

The four dissenters on the right, meanwhile, left no doubt that they were ready to plunge ahead toward greater limits on the power of the Federal Government. "The fragmentation of power produced by the structure of our government," they wrote, "is central to liberty, and when we destroy it, we place liberty at peril." Their rare jointly written opinion encouraged speculation, later supported by leaked accounts of the Justices' discussions, that Roberts had jumped ship from his conservative colleagues at the last minute; his "verbal wizardry," they seethed, went "deep into the forbidden land of the sophists." Their preference would have been to strike down the entire 2,400-page law, every word of it, and let slip the dogs of war. Instead, the Chief Justice decided to give peace a chance. ∎

—*By David Von Drehle*

**In the arena** *Roberts found himself in the crosshairs as the Court ruled on the Affordable Care Act*

# John Roberts

The Chief Justice of the United States crafts a compromise

**C**HIEF JUSTICE JOHN ROBERTS ARRIVED AT the Supreme Court in 2005 full of promises to dial down the partisan rhetoric and foster the court's reputation as a fair-minded forum, not a food fight. He has not always succeeded. Yet when Roberts, a handsome guy of 57 raised in upstate New York and small-town Indiana, took his seat at the center of the bench on June 28, 2012. the final day of the court's term, and declared himself the fifth and deciding vote to uphold President Obama's health-care reform initiative, the Affordable Care Act, he showed himself a Chief Justice with a sense of history—and a willingness, rare today, to seek common ground and compromise. By and large the Chiefs who fare well down the years are the ones who prove effective politicians, judges who understand that the Supreme Court is a fundamentally political institution whose standing with the nation is fluid, not fixed.

It may be hard to believe, but generations of Americans considered compromise an admirable quality. Schoolteachers taught their students about the Great Compromise that produced the Constitution, and about the Missouri Compromise that—for a time—held it together. Now the word connotes something bad. A leaky gasket has been "compromised," and cheating spouses are caught in "compromising" positions. What Roberts managed to do with Obamacare vindicated the virtue of compromise in an era of Occupiers, Tea Partyers and litmus-testing special interests.

The Chief Justice didn't seek some nonexistent middle ground halfway between irreconcilable poles. He found a means of giving both sides just enough of what they wanted that he was able to avert a crisis. In the superheated conflict mill that is American politics in 2012, it's good to have someone in a position of authority willing to try.

What's more, Roberts found a way through that did not betray his own firmly held beliefs. The Roman Catholic was conservative more than 30 years ago, when he clerked for the future Chief Justice William

Rehnquist, and conservative when he served as a counsel in the Reagan White House. He was conservative when his name appeared in a leadership directory of the Federalist Society, and he is still conservative today. He managed to stand well above the toxic cloud of partisan rancor that has settled over the capital, making him perhaps the healthiest figure, politically speaking, in government. After seven terms as Chief Justice, he finally put the *Roberts* in the Roberts Court.

John Q. Barrett, a law professor at St. John's University, described the ruling as a classic example of a cautious Chief Justice at work. "I think that Chiefs feel, for the public credibility and independence of the court, that major legislation should not be struck down on a 5-to-4 vote on grounds that Congress lacks the power. It hasn't happened in the modern era—since the 1930s. John Roberts will likely be Chief Justice for many, many more years, and it's not surprising to me that he wasn't looking to define his court stewardship with a radical decision. The opposite ruling would have been a deeply, permanently controversial landmark."

Ultimately, Roberts brought the court down squarely on the side of one of the most basic conservative principles of all: that big decisions in the U.S. should be made not by judges or bureaucrats but by voters. "The Framers created a Federal Government of limited powers, and assigned to this Court the duty of enforcing those limits. The Court does so today," he wrote at the end of his decision. "But the Court does not express any opinion on the wisdom of the Affordable Care Act. Under the Constitution, that judgment is reserved to the people ... It is so ordered." ■

—By Jon Meacham and David Von Drehle

## Roberts found a means of giving both sides just enough of what they wanted that he was able to avert a crisis

STEVE PYKE—CONTOUR/GETTY IMAGES

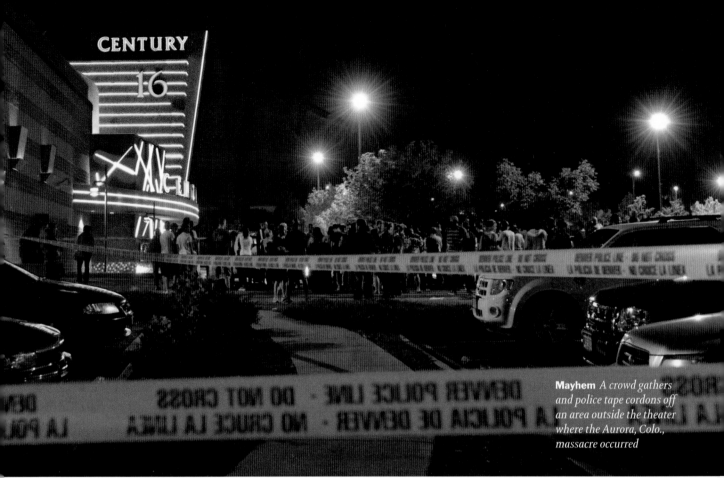

**Mayhem** *A crowd gathers and police tape cordons off an area outside the theater where the Aurora, Colo., massacre occurred*

THIS PAGE, FROM TOP: KARL GEHRING—DENVER POST/AP; DENVER POST/POLARIS; RIGHT PAGE, FROM LEFT: BARRY GUTIEREZ/AP; SCOTT OLSON—GETTY IMAGES

CRIME

# Senseless Deeds

## Mass murderers assault moviegoers in a Colorado theater and worshippers at a Sikh temple in Wisconsin

THEY THOUGHT HE WAS PART OF THE show. When James Holmes stepped through an exit door into a movie auditorium in Aurora, Colo., a Denver suburb where the premiere of the last film in director Christopher Nolan's popular Batman series, *The Dark Knight Rises,* was showing on the night of Thursday, July 19, the audience members nearby took him for one of those fans who arrive at a multiplex dressed as a favorite character from the movie they've come to see. Outfitted in a gas mask and Kevlar suit, toting an assault rifle and a Remington 870 shotgun, Holmes, 24, bore a resemblance to Bane, the gaudiest villain of the much-anticipated action film. But he was not the costumed surrogate of the audience. Holmes proceed-

**Holmes**

ed to do what Bane does in the film: invade a public place and terrorize the people in it. He was a surrogate for the violence on the screen— Bane for real.

Holmes set off tear-gas grenades and began firing at the crowd. By the time his rampage was over and he had left the theater, 12 people were dead and 58 had been wounded, some seriously. Some bullets went through the walls between auditoriums to strike viewers in the adjacent theater. Arriving on the scene, police found Holmes with a mask, a rifle and a handgun by a car behind the multiplex. Two more firearms, another assault weapon and another handgun, were found inside his vehicle.

Holmes did not resist arrest; he told officers after being

38

taken into custody that he had booby-trapped his apartment and that he was the Joker, Batman's fictional nemesis. Police disarmed an explosive device and entered the young man's apartment, where they found an arsenal of weapons, more than 30 homemade grenades and 10 gal. of gasoline—as well as a Batman mask and poster.

When Holmes entered a courtroom on July 23 to be arraigned, his hair was dyed a bright orange color and he appeared dazed; in the weeks that followed, more of his story came to light. The Ph.D. student in neuroscience at the University of Colorado Anschutz Medical Campus in Aurora had graduated with honors from the University of California, Riverside, in 2010 but had dropped out of his classes in Aurora in June 2012 after failing an exam. Fellow students recalled having been concerned about his mental state as his classroom performance declined. It was also learned that Holmes had begun acquiring his large personal arsenal of weapons in the spring of 2012.

On July 30, Colorado prosecutors formally charged Holmes with a staggering number of crimes, including 24 counts of first-degree murder (two per victim), 116 counts of attempted murder and possession of explosive devices. Holmes' court-appointed attorneys maintained that the young man was mentally ill. As of early October 2012, Holmes was awaiting trial, and the grieving citizens of Aurora, joined by many other Americans, were left to question their fellow citizens' clear preference to continue to offer easy access to guns for wildlife sportsmen, cautious homeowners and murderous psychopaths. ■

**Comfort** *Judy Goos, left, hugs family friend Isaiah Bow, 20, who survived the theater attack, as Terrell Wallin, 20, right, looks on*

## In Wisconsin, a Deadly Attack at a Sikh Temple

Police were called to the peaceful confines of Sikh Temple of Wisconsin in the Milwaukee suburb of Oak Creek on Sunday morning, Aug. 5, after a lone gunman entered the facility and opened fire on congregants who were preparing for the weekly service. Witnesses described taking cover in a variety of locations inside the temple complex as the killer stalked his victims. Six Sikhs were killed and three people wounded before the gunman shot himself.

The dead assailant was Wade Michael Page, 40, a longtime advocate of white supremacy and a member of several bands in the underground white power music scene. Page had been involuntarily discharged from the U.S. Army in 1998 and had legally purchased the handgun used in the killings a week before his rampage.

The murders shocked the Sikh community in the U.S., which numbers about 700,000, as well as the worldwide faithful. Sikhism, founded in the 16th century, is based in Amritsar, India. The fifth largest religion in the world, it preaches universal brotherhood and advocates meditation. After the shootings, many male U.S. Sikhs, who are easily distinguished by their flowing beards and turbans, described a notable increase in prejudice against them in the years since the terrorist attacks of 9/11, noting that many Americans mistakenly believe that Sikhs are Muslims.

Thousands of Sikhs from around the world attended an Aug. 10 memorial service for the victims of the rampage in Oak Creek, where U.S. Attorney General Eric Holder declared, "In the recent past, too many Sikhs have been targeted, victimized simply because of who they are, how they look and what they believe."

# In Brief

## Dream Act, Obama Edition

**IMMIGRATION** Acting decisively on an issue long bottled up by partisan gridlock in Congress—the immigration bill known as the Dream Act, first proposed in 2001—President Barack Obama announced on June 15 that by Executive Order, the Administration would stop deporting many young undocumented immigrants in the U.S. The announcement was clearly timed to sway Latino voters to the President's side during an election year. Over the past three years, Obama had faced attacks from Latinos for not doing more to push immigration reform, either by forcing the Dream Act or other measures through a recalcitrant Congress or by embracing Executive Branch options instead.

On Aug. 15, the first day the new program, Deferred Action for Childhood Arrivals, began accepting applications, thousands of undocumented young people lined up across the country to file claims to avoid deportation and obtain the right to work. Critics, including Arizona Governor Jan Brewer, strongly opposed the measure, claiming it would only act to increase the flow of illegal immigrants into the U.S. In TIME, former Bush Administration official Karen Hughes called the move "a raw display of political power ... worthy of the best of Chicago's political machine."

## Walker Wins In Wisconsin

**STATEHOUSES** Concluding a long-running face-off that rocked the state of Wisconsin, Republican Governor Scott Walker, 44, survived a June 5 recall election, beating Milwaukee mayor Tom Barrett 53% to 46%.

Early in 2011, Walker proposed restricting the collective-bargaining rights of some of the state's public unions, sparking major protests. The GOP-led legislature passed the measure on March 10, 2011, and in November 2011 Walker's opponents launched the petition drive that forced the recall election.

## Crime and Punishment

**LAW** Two high-profile criminal cases made headlines in 2012: the child-molestation trial of onetime Penn State University assistant football coach Jerry Sandusky, and the killing of an unarmed black Florida teen by a local neighborhood watch captain.

### Pennsylvania: Sandusky Is Jailed

Jerry Sandusky, 68, who served for 30 years as an assistant under legendary head football coach Joe Paterno at Penn State, was at the center of the case that brought Paterno's heralded career to a ruinous end. Accused of failing to investigate allegations that Sandusky had molested children on university grounds, Paterno was fired by Penn State in November 2011; he died in January 2012.

On June 22, Sandusky was found guilty of 45 of 48 charges of sexual abuse of minors over a period of 15 years. On Oct. 9 he was sentenced to serve 30 to 60 years in prison. His lawyers plan to appeal.

### Florida: Homicide or Self-defense?

Trayvon Martin, 17, a black high school student, was walking through a largely white area of Sanford, Fla., near Orlando, on Feb. 26, when he was approached by a suspicious neighborhood watch captain, Hispanic-American George Zimmerman, 28. After an altercation, the unarmed Martin was shot dead by Zimmerman, who told police Martin had accosted him. Zimmerman was not arrested, per Florida's Stand Your Ground law, which justifies self-defense, but after a national outcry, he was charged with murder in April. He was released on a $1 million bond and will stand trial in 2013.

CLOCKWISE FROM TOP LEFT: JACK KURTZ—ZUMA PRESS; NABIL K. MARK—CENTRE DAILY TIMES/AP; PAUL HENNESSY—POLARIS; MORRY GASH—AP

CLOCKWISE FROM TOP: SCOTT OLSON—GETTY IMAGES; JUSTIN SULLIVAN—GETTY IMAGES; SITHIXAY DITTHAVONG—AP

## After 11 Years, America's War in Afghanistan Begins to Wind Down

**DEFENSE** *Above, soldiers from the 713th Engineer Company of the Indiana Army National Guard are greeted by family members in Gary, Ind., on Sept. 26, after their return from Afghanistan. The withdrawal of U.S. forces from the Asian nation accelerated in the final months of 2012, and is scheduled to conclude in 2014. In a troubling new trend, U.S. and NATO soldiers were killed by gunfire from Afghan security personnel at least 40 times in 2012 alone, as Americans continued to lose faith in the widely discredited regime of Hamid Karzai, and Taliban forces seemed to gain strength. As of late 2012, the war has continued for 11 years; in August it claimed its 2,000th American combat casualty. Polls showed a majority of Americans favor ending U.S. and NATO operations in the troubled nation.*

## Teachers Strike in Chicago

**EDUCATION** More than 26,000 teachers and support staff of Chicago's public schools walked out on strike on Monday, Sept. 10, for the first time in 25 years, after 10 months of negotiations failed to yield a contract. The action by the Chicago Teachers Union left 350,000 students in the nation's third largest school system idle.

After seven days without classes, an agreement was reached that will require the school district to fill half of all job openings with laid-off teachers and will limit the portion of teachers' evaluations that are tied to student performance to the bare minimum required by a new state law. Long-running negotiations in Boston also ended with a new contract for teachers in September.

**NUMBERS**

# $44,000

*Estimated hourly pay of Simon Property Group's David Simon, the highest-paid CEO of a public company in the U.S. Simon was paid $137 million in 2011*

# $750 BILLION

*Amount wasted each year in the U.S. health-care system, mainly on unneeded care, unnecessary tests, complicated paperwork and fraud, according to the independent non-profit organization the Institute of Medicine*

## A Wave of Bankrupt Cities

**CITIES** On June 28, 2012, Stockton, Calif., became the largest city in U.S. history to file for protection under Chapter 9 bankruptcy laws. "In recent years this inland port city of nearly 300,000 people has earned several distinctions, none of them good," Jason Motlagh wrote in TIME. "Twice atop *Forbes'* list of America's Most Miserable Cities ... Second highest violent-crime rate in California ... Second highest home-foreclosure rate of all major U.S. metro areas."

Current city officials blamed not only the national recession and crash in housing prices but also reckless spending on public-employee contracts by prior civic leaders; the city's long-term health-care costs alone amount to more than $400 million. Stockton was only the most notable of a number of cities that filed for bankruptcy around the nation in 2012.

# World

FROM LEFT: SERGEY PONOMAREV—AP; MUHAMMAD ADIMAJA—
DEMOTIX/CORBIS; KNS/AFP/GETTYIMAGES

"We can say whatever we want. Their mouths are sewn shut."
—Nadezdha Tolokonnikova, member of Pussy Riot, referring to her prosecutors and judges

# Agents of Outrage

## Four Americans die when the Middle East explodes with rage

IN THE DAYS FOLLOWING SEPT. 11, 2012, THE 11TH anniversary of 9/11, many nations of the Islamic world were convulsed by violent protests against the U.S. From Cairo to Jakarta, from Jordan to Pakistan, anti-American demonstrators paraded through the streets of major cities, often ending their march at U.S. embassies, where they vented their disgust with a highly partisan film made in the U.S. that mocked the Prophet Muhammad. Amid the global uproar, U.S. Ambassador Chris Stevens and three other Americans were killed in an attack on the U.S. consulate in Benghazi, Libya—the city in which Stevens and other Americans had helped Libyan rebels direct the campaign that led to the downfall of the dictator Colonel Muammar Gaddafi in 2011.

MOISES SAIMAN—MAGNUM FOR TIME

**Aftermath** *Angered by an anti-Islamic video made in the U.S., Egyptians hurl rocks at the U.S. embassy in Cairo*

re-evaluation of events became an issue in itself, magnified amid the heat of the U.S. presidential campaign.

**Instigating anger** The tale of these events, then, is really two stories. The first begins with the reaction to the video, which TIME editor-at-large Bobby Ghosh described as "the product of a sequence of provocations, some mysterious, some obvious." The cast of characters in this tragedy included a shadowy filmmaker, a sinister pastor in Florida, an Egyptian-American Islamophobe, an Egyptian TV host and politically powerful Islamist extremist groups in a host of Islamic lands. The instigators and executors didn't work in concert, Ghosh noted; they probably didn't even know they were in cahoots. But they needed one another to fan the flames of hatred.

Collectively, these hatemongers form a global industry of outrage, working feverishly to give and take offense, frequently over religion, and to ignite the combustible mix of ignorance and suspicion that exists almost as much in the U.S. as in the Arab world. Add to this combination the presence of opportunistic jihadist groups seeking to capitalize on any mayhem that develops, and you can begin to connect the dots between a tawdry little film and U.S. diplomats under siege in the Muslim world.

The trail begins with the filmmaker behind *Innocence of Muslims,* a purported biopic of the Prophet Muhammad. He went by a number of names, but he turned out to be an Egyptian Copt, Mark Basseley Youssef, living in the U.S., with a history of convictions for deeds including drug possession and bank fraud. In recent years, Youssef had become an increasingly active Islamophobe. In the wake of the events he helped author, Youssef was arrested for eight probation violations on Sept. 27, 2012.

The zealot's film, apparently made in 2011, was designed to insult Islam and provoke hatred of it. Its slanders of the Prophet are rehashed from old Islamophobic tropes; the script is clunky and the acting high-schoolish. Most offensive of all to Muslims: the film dares to show Muhammad himself, defying one of the most sacred strictures of Islam.

The film was screened in Hollywood in mid-2012, but fewer than 10 people attended. Youssef then posted a 14-min. series of clips on YouTube in July that caught the eye of Morris Sadek, an Egyptian-American Copt in Washington, D.C., known for incendiary anti-Muslim views. He gave the video the oxygen of publicity, attracting a singularly unattractive fan: Terry Jones, a Florida pastor notorious for burning the Koran and performing

Americans recoiled in horror at the attacks. Yet as it turned out, the events of 9/11/12 were by no means as simple as they first appeared. In fact, the outrage over the video was far from spontaneous: it was, rather, the anticipated outcome of a series of provocations by extremists in both the U.S. and the Middle East whose agenda is to spread hatred. More important, the attack on the U.S. consulate in Benghazi, originally viewed as part of the widespread response to the video, was later determined to be not a spontaneous protest by irate citizens but rather a deliberate attack by a terrorist group (or groups) striking at the U.S. on the anniversary of 9/11. The tardiness with which the Obama Administration announced this

other Islamophobic stunts. Jones further publicized the film, and soon the thread was picked up in Egypt by a TV host every bit as inflammatory and opportunistic as Jones: Sheik Khaled Abdallah of the Islamist satellite-TV station al-Nas. He assailed the video, triggering the next domino to fall. The Salafists, a fundamentalist Islamic movement that makes up the second largest faction in the Egyptian Parliament, had been staging protests outside the U.S. embassy in Cairo for months; the offensive film gave them a fresh reason to do so.

Youssef's match had found a combustible agent. In Cairo on Sept. 11, some 1,500 protesters, many of them Salafists, gathered outside the walls of the heavily fortified U.S. embassy, lustily shouting anti-American slogans. Some protesters scaled the wall surrounding the citadel-like embassy that sits just off Tahrir Square. They made no move to enter or damage embassy buildings, but they did remove the American flag from a pole that stood just inside the embassy walls and replaced it with a black flag bearing the slogan "There is no God but God, and Muhammad is his messenger." Egyptian security forces,

hopelessly outnumbered, mostly just watched. The crowd eventually dispersed—but the lax security effort by Egyptian police was the subject of a blistering phone call that President Obama put in to Egypt's President Mohamed Morsi after the embassy was breached.

Around the world, the story was similar: protesters demonstrated outside U.S. embassies, burned U.S. flags and chanted anti-American slogans. Often lost in the uproar was a key point: the protests were staged by small groups of extremists rather than by large groups of diverse citizens. As Egyptian journalist Ashraf Khalil wrote in TIME shortly after the attack, "The term "storming"—deployed in initial breathless media reports—is probably a little strong for what took place in Cairo ... This was essentially a case of an American group of fringe Christian fundamentalists successfully provoking and enraging a similar group of fringe Muslim fundamentalists."

**Attack in Benghazi** The events at Benghazi were originally viewed as yet another of the anti-video protests. Instead, it gradually emerged, they were the result of a

## Tough Questions About Benghazi

The deaths of Ambassador Chris Stevens and three other Americans in Libya at the hands of terrorists reverberated around the world in the days and weeks after Sept. 11, 2012. The tragedy put the Obama Administration on the defensive in the waning weeks of a presidential election, with critics assailing the State Department for not providing sufficient security at the consulate in Benghazi (shown above on the night of Sept. 11), and sharply questioning the Administration's changing accounts of the events.

Although President Obama denounced "acts of terror" the day after the incident and in a campaign speech on the following day, U.S. Ambassador to the

U.N. Susan Rice declared on Sept. 16, "We do not have information at present that leads us to conclude that this was premeditated or preplanned." Yet only three days later, Matthew Olsen, director of the National Counterterrorism Center, told a Senate committee that the Americans "were killed in the course of a terrorist attack on our embassy," referring to the consulate.

On Oct. 10, the House Committee on Oversight and Government Reform convened hearings, and Republican members grilled four officials about the events in Benghazi and security preparations on the ground. South Carolina Congressman Trey Gowdy, noting the changing accounts of the incident, declared, "I want to know why we were lied to." For their part, Democrats pointed out that House Republicans had voted twice in the past two years to reduce funding for security at U.S. embassies.

As the clamor mounted, Secretary of State Hillary Clinton declared on Oct. 15 that she took full responsibility for the incident. In the presidential debate the following night, President Obama claimed that he, as Clinton's superior, bore the responsibility for the events. When challenger Mitt Romney questioned whether the Administration had perhaps tried to mislead Americans about the events, however, the President bristled and described his remarks as "offensive." The last word on the subject would be in the hands of American voters.

coordinated terrorist attack by a jihadist group or groups. As Charlene Lamb of the State Department later testified to a U.S. House committee, "The attack began at approximately 9:40 p.m. local time ... Dozens of attackers ... launched a full-scale assault that was unprecedented in its size and intensity." The attackers were using rocket-propelled grenades, proof that they were far from everyday protesters. They successfully breached the gates of the consulate and set fire to its buildings, as U.S. security personnel returned fire and attempted to shelter both Ambassador Stevens, 52, and information management officer Sean Smith, 34. But the men became separated amid the ongoing combat and heavy smoke. When the secruity agents located Smith's body in the consulate's Tactical Operations Center, he had died from smoke inhalation.

Ambassador Stevens had not been located when U.S. personnel evacuated the consulate grounds in an armored vehicle, fleeing to a nearby "safe" compound about a half-mile away. It was during this time that Stevens' body was found, perhaps by looters, and taken to a hospital, where he was pronounced dead by smoke inhalation. About 1:30 a.m., a rescue team of eight U.S. special security officers arrived in Benghazi from Tripoli, the capital. They met up at the safe house with the personnel who had evacuated the consulate. The safe house was subsequently attacked by grenades and was hit by at least two mortar rounds. It was during this firefight that two former U.S. Navy SEALs who were working as security personnel in Libya, Tyrone Woods and Glen Doherty, were killed and two U.S. military officers were severely wounded.

The anti-U.S. protests triggered by the Islamophobic video were troubling but not unexpected. In contrast, the deaths of Ambassador Stevens and three other Americans will be studied closely to ensure that such events are never repeated. As TIME's Ghosh noted, "The Arab Spring replaced the harsh order of hated dictators with a flowering of neophyte democracies. But these governments—with weak mandates, ever shifting loyalties and poor security forces—have made the region a more chaotic and unstable place, a place more susceptible than ever to rogue provocateurs fomenting violent upheavals, usually in the name of faith." Defeating the agents of outrage may be the work of decades, but it is work that must be done. ■

## "It is especially tragic that Chris Stevens died in Benghazi, because it is a city that he helped to save."

—PRESIDENT BARACK OBAMA

## Chris Stevens, 1960-2012

*Salaam alaikum.* My name is Chris Stevens, and I'm the new U.S. Ambassador to Libya." With those words Christopher Stevens—the diplomat who was killed along with three other Americans in the attack on the U.S. consulate in Benghazi, Libya—began an online video introducing himself to the people of Libya. Though he took up his position only in May, he wasn't new to the region. An Arabic and French speaker, Stevens, 52, on the right above with Libyan Justice Minister Ali Ashour, had been a Peace Corps volunteer in Morocco. After working in international trade law in Washington, he served in Israel, Egypt and Saudi Arabia during his 21 years with the State Department.

But it was in Libya where Stevens made his mark. His experience and credibility in a country that had long been off-limits proved invaluable during the chaotic Libyan revolution, and his work helped persuade the Obama Administration to provide conclusive support to the besieged rebels. That made Stevens' death all the more ironic—as President Barack Obama said after the attacks, "It is especially tragic that Chris Stevens died in Benghazi, because it is a city that he helped to save."

It's telling that less than three hours after Stevens' death, Libyans had started an Arabic-language Facebook tribute page for him. The next week, thousands of Libyans took to the streets of Benghazi to honor him. The marchers laid siege to the complexes of Islamic militant groups, forcing some militia members to flee. The pro-U.S. marchers far outnumbered the few jihadists who had murdered Chris Stevens.

LEFT: MUSTAFA EL-SHRIDI—EPA/CORBIS. RIGHT: ANIS MILI—REUTERS

# Syria Burning

Locked in a civil war of relentless attrition, the Middle Eastern nation self-immolates, with no end in sight

**T**HE ITALIAN LEFTIST ANTONIO GRAMSCI MAY have been writing from inside Mussolini's prisons in the 1930s, but he could have been describing today's Syria when he noted that revolutionary crises are moments in which "the old is dying, and the new cannot be born," and are characterized by a "great variety of morbid symptoms." Throughout 2012 Syria was a charnel house of morbid symptoms, as the regime's army and its many foes clashed from house to house on the streets of its largest cities, in villages across the countryside and along Syria's borders with neighboring states.

On one side of this war was ruthless President Bashar Assad, 47, and his army of more than 200,000 men, tanks, mortars and weapons from Russia. Opposing them was a loose confederation of lightly armed military defectors and, in some areas, civilians, who were waging a growing number of guerrilla campaigns in their hometowns and cities. Several competing groups claimed to speak for all the rebel forces, but Assad's opponents were neither organized nor unified, unlike the Benghazi-based National Transitional Council of Libya, which led the united front that brought down the regime of Colonel Muammar Gaddafi in 2011 with aid from the U.S. and NATO.

Trapped in the middle were the people of Syria, a di-

MANU BRABO—AP

verse nation of 23 million citizens, who have chafed under the harsh rule of the Assad family for 32 years. Those now rising up against the regime knew they could expect no leniency from Bashar Assad: when the city of Hama rebelled against the rule of his father Hafez Assad in 1982, the autocrat sent in tanks and artillery to pound the city into surrender, at a cost of some 20,000 lives. As Syrian troops bombarded the nation's cities in 2012, it was clear that Bashar Assad was cast in the mold of his father.

Unlike the rebels in Libya, Syria's anti-Assad warriors had no reason to expect aid from the outside world. Western powers had no appetite for direct military involve-

ment in Syria, not only because of post-Iraq, Afghanistan and Libya intervention fatigue, but also because the sectarian and regional political stakes in Syria's conflict threatened regionwide chaos. Support for direct military intervention appeared to be lacking even when the proposed fighters were not Western troops: twice in 2012, Qatar failed in its efforts to persuade other Arab nations in the Persian Gulf to back intervention by an Arab force

**Up in flames** *Smoke rises over the battered Saif al-Dawla quarter of Aleppo on Oct. 2, 2012, where forces loyal to Syrian President Bashar Assad were clashing with rebel militias*

49

**Molotov cocktail** *A rebel soldier throws a petrol bomb toward Syrian army positions in Aleppo on Oct. 3, 2012*

that would invade Syria to open humanitarian corridors to besieged cities.

Bashar Assad was threatened in 2012, but he remained in power, enjoying strong backing from longtime allies Russia and Iran, while countries such as China and Iraq insisted that any solution in Syria be based on diplomatic reforms and dialogue with the Assad regime, rather than its replacement. In a February show of strength, even as Assad's forces were raining artillery fire down on the rebel stronghold of Homs in Syria's west, the regime staged an election and won voter approval for a package of constitutional reforms. Opposition leaders called the vote a farce, yet Western journalists in the major cities of Damascus and Aleppo saw thousands of young voters lining up to vote in spite of opposition calls for a boycott.

**Summer battles** Assad's showcase referendum was a reminder that his regime retained a substantial base of supporters, with a number of key constituencies fearful of their prospects, should the rebellion triumph—in particular the Alawites, a Shi'ite Muslim sect that dominates key military units, as well as Christians and other minorities that make up as much as a third of the population.

Yet throughout the summer the rebels demonstrated their own growing strength. Early in July, Assad's regime was rocked by two high-profile defections—top military man General Manaf Tlass and former ambassador to Iraq Nawaf al-Fares. Their exit prompted headlines suggesting the regime was nearing collapse. Both men were among the most senior Sunni figures of the regime, as had been all 13 generals who jumped ship before them. In the cauldron of war, Islamic sectarianism was eradicating the tolerance for diversity that once characterized Syria.

In another rebel success, on July 18 a bomb blast at the national security headquarters in Damascus killed Defense Minister Daoud Rajiha and deputy army chief Assef Shawkat, who was also President Assad's brother-in-law. The bombing prompted days of continuous fighting involving armor and artillery that rattled the capital city.

**"The military is still loyal to Assad, despite a very big wave of defections, and he and his family are still in Damascus."**

—ISRAELI MILITARY SPOKESMAN

"It happened in the most guarded neighborhood inside Damascus, very close to where Bashar and his mother and other family members are, and where there are many intelligence locations," retired Syrian Brigadier General Akil Hashem, who lives in exile in Paris, told TIME. "The regime is collapsing from inside."

Or not: the rebel forces were soon driven out and order was restored in Damascus, while reports that Assad had fled the capital proved false. "The military is still loyal to Assad, despite a very big wave of defections, and he and his family are still in Damascus," a spokesman for the Israeli military declared.

Meanwhile, British-sponsored attempts at the U.N. to enact tough new sanctions against Damascus failed on July 19, when both Russia and China vetoed the proposal in the Security Council. On Aug. 2, former U.N. Secretary General Kofi Annan resigned his post as U.N. special envoy to the region, having failed to win Assad's support for his proposed peace plan. On the ground, the opposition forces remained deeply divided, with dozens of rival militias fighting under autonomous commanders. To further complicate matters, the rebel armies were welcoming a growing number of foreign jihadist militants, causing increasing discomfort among Western governments.

In the fall the conflict moved into a new phase, as a wave of intense fighting rocked the streets of Aleppo, the nation's largest city and its commercial and financial hub. As rebels mounted furious attacks, Assad's forces bombed residential neighborhoods, proving that he was prepared to destroy the port city in order to "save it."

**Forecast: more misery** By November 2012, after 20 months of fighting, at a cost of an estimated 30,000 lives, the conflict in Syria appeared to be settling into a strategic stalemate, with neither side capable of destroying the other, while the body count kept rising steadily in a brutal war of attrition, and the nation's infrastructure deteriorated.

The more optimistic observers in the West imagined a situation in which the regime, unable to restore control over vast swaths of territory, found itself starved by sanctions until Assad's power eroded to the point of collapse. Pessimists in the West saw the makings of a repeat of Lebanon's 17-year civil war in the 1970s and '80s, in which the country, and even the capital city, deteriorated into warring fiefdoms held by various religious sects—backed by competing regional powers—that were able to maintain their standoff for years on end. As in Lebanon in the '80s, the pessimists feared, Syria's old order was dying, its new order could not be born, and its morbid interlude showed every sign of proving to be a protracted one. ∎

*—By Tony Karon, Rania Abouzeid and Pelin Turgut*

LEFT: MANU BRABO—AP. RIGHT: SANA SANA—REUTERS

## Assad: Man in the Middle

Syria's President, Bashar Assad, who has ruled his nation since 2000, found himself in 2012 at the center of a conflict that was destabilizing the entire Middle East. Turkey, Syria's neighbor to the north, actively supported the rebels, as did Saudi Arabia and other Sunni states of the Gulf; Shi'ite Iran backed Assad.

In July, Syria downed a Turkish fighter jet that Ankara said was on a training flight in international airspace, killing its two pilots. Turkey subsequently reinforced its border with anti-aircraft missiles and threatened to target any approaching Syrian military elements. Many Turks believed that an upsurge in attacks by the Kurdish separatist Kurdistan Workers' Party insurgents in Turkey's southeast reflected Assad's response to Turkey's support for his overthrow. Some 100,000 refugees from Syria were living in camps in Turkey near the border.

By October, Syrian and Turkish forces were shelling each other across the border. On Oct. 3, five civilians in Turkey were killed by mortar shells fired from Syria, and Turkish President Recep Tayyip Erdogan quickly pushed a bill through Parliament authorizing his armed forces to conduct operations across the border.

Syria's neighbor to the south, Jordan, was also feeling the heat. On Oct. 10, U.S. Secretary of Defense Leon Panetta declared he was sending a contingent of U.S. special forces to Jordan, noting that some 200,000 Syrians had fled into that nation and citing the possible hazard should the Assad regime's large supplies of chemical weapons become a factor in the civil war.

# Growing Pains. China spars with Japan and welcomes new leaders

## A WAR OF WATER CANNONS—FOR NOW

Above, sailors strike a pose aboard China's first aircraft carrier, the *Liaoning*. The ship is not a new one: it is a renovated Soviet-era craft purchased from Ukraine, but it showcases China's ongoing attempts to project its power into Asian sealanes.

That effort accelerated in September, when Chinese vessels repeatedly entered territorial waters around the Senkaku Islands (the Diaoyu Islands, to the Chinese), a group of uninhabited islands in the East China Sea claimed by China, Japan and Taiwan but now administered by Japan. At right, a Japanese coast guard vessel (at bottom) exchanges water-cannon volleys with a cruiser from Taiwan off the Senkakus in September, even as large government-sponsored protests in Beijing attacked Japan's claims to the islands.

The U.S. did not take sides in the dispute in its early weeks, but the Senkakus fall under the U.S.-Japan security treaty, which would require the U.S. to come to Japan's aid in case of attack. A U.S. Navy fleet sped to the region in late September.

FROM TOP: ZHA CHUNMING—XINHUA PRESS/CORBIS; THE ASAHI SHIMBUN/GETTY IMAGES

## WORKERS RIOT AT A FOXCONN PLANT

The harsh working conditions in China's high-tech, high-pressure factories have long been a source of concern. At right, tensions boiled over on the evening of Sept. 23 at a Foxconn assembly plant in the northern city of Taiyuan, where 79,000 workers toil. Thousands of employees clashed with security police, closing down the assembly lines of the world's largest maker of electronics, which builds devices for the likes of Apple, Nokia and Sony. More demonstrations followed in October.

Taiwan-owned Foxconn employs some 1 million people across China; earlier criticism had led Apple to request an audit of the manufacturer's practices by independent monitoring agency the Fair Labor Association.

## A BRITON DIES, AND A POLITICAL DYNASTY FALLS

A complex crime story involving fast-rising Chinese party official Bo Xilai, his wife and a murdered British businessman electrified China in 2012. Bo, 63, below left, was Chonqing's boss and China's most charismatic local leader; he had won fame for championing a return to Maoist philosophies.

The scandal began with the murder of Neil Heywood, a Briton who died in a Chongqing hotel room in 2011. Suspicion fell on Gu Kailai, 53, Bo's wife, after Bo's top aide, Wang Lijun, sought sanctuary in a U.S. consulate in nearby Chengdu and accused the two of Heywood's murder and other crimes. On Aug. 9, Gu was convicted of poisoning Heywood after a brief trial, above, in which she was said to have confessed her guilt. She was given a suspended death sentence.

Bo lost his Chonqing position in April. On Sept. 28 he was expelled from the party and charged with abusing his power, accepting massive bribes and other crimes. The scandal roiled the national party's plans to conduct a smooth leadership transition.

## A CONFUSED TRANSFER OF POWER

For years now, China's ruling Communist Party has kept the nation's economy surging, even as its citizens demanded more freedoms. In 2012 the strain of sustaining equilibrium began to show, as political bosses fell, workers rioted and the once-a-decade transition to a new leadership team threatened to come apart at the seams.

At the center of the storm was intended new party boss Xi Jinping, 59, below, who disappeared from view for two weeks in September, even as the early-November transition loomed. Xi's absence was not explained by authorities, and it raised questions about the orderliness of the transition and the extent of Xi's grasp on power.

CLOCKWISE FROM TOP: IMAGINECHINA; LARRY DOWNING—AP; WENG LEI—IMAGINECHINA; ANDY WONG—AP

# Kim Jong Un

## Will an untested new leader turn North Korea's face to the West?

**N**ORTH KOREA IS A COCKTAIL OF POISONOUS elements: autocratic, repressive, isolated and poor. Its regime is dangerous not only to its people but also to the rest of the world. North Korea, notes South Korean scholar Cheong Seong Chang, is "a Stalinist monarchy" in which bloodlines, and only bloodlines, determine who the next dictator will be—no matter how inexperienced that person may be.

Nearly 30,000 U.S. troops help defend the North's prosperous, democratic brethren in the South against a 1.2 million-member army. Over the past decade, despite crippling economic sanctions imposed by most of the outside world, North Korea has defiantly developed and tested nuclear weapons and the long-range missiles needed to deliver them. Western intelligence agencies estimate that Pyongyang possesses eight to 12 nuclear weapons. The hard truth is that North Korea is Asia's last remaining cold war trip wire.

This is the country now ostensibly helmed by Kim Jong Un, nearing 30 by most accounts, the grandson of Kim Il Sung, the founder of the Democratic People's Republic of Korea (DPRK). When he died in 1994, his eldest son, Kim Jong Il, then 52, continued the dynasty. With Kim Jong Il's death in December 2011 at age 69, it was Kim Jong Un's turn.

Kim Jong Un was Kim Jong Il's third son and the second with his consort, Ko Young Hui, an ethnic Korean born in Osaka, Japan, who died in 2004 of breast cancer. She and her family had returned to North Korea in the early '60s, when Japanese-born Koreans were the lowest of the low in North Korea's quasi-caste system. But Ko, a dancer, caught the eye of the "Dear Leader." Around 1981 she gave birth to a boy, Kim Jong Chul; Kim Jong Un was born two years later. In the mid-1990s, like his older male siblings, Kim Jong Un moved to Switzerland. He stayed with a family assigned to the North Korean embassy in Bern and for the first two years of his life there studied German and English. In 1998, under the pseudonym Pak Un and the pretext of being the son of a diplomat, he enrolled in seventh grade at Schule Liebefeld-Stein-hölzli, a public school in the suburb of Liebefeld.

Despite the deception surrounding his identity, the boy lived a normal life. He stayed in a nondescript apartment block about a 10-minute walk from school, and he began a love affair with U.S. basketball. At a time when Michael Jordan was dominating the NBA, Kim became a big fan of the Chicago Bulls, says one-time classmate Joao Micaelo, now a chef in Vienna.

In 2000, just after he had started ninth grade, Kim left school abruptly and headed back home. For much of the next decade, his life is even more of a blank, other than the fact that he attended the Kim Il Sung Military Academy in Pyongyang (senior-thesis topic: guidance systems for artillery).

When Kim Jong Il suffered a stroke in 2008, Un's older brother Kim Jong Chul was most often cited as the likely heir, given that Kim Jong Nam, the eldest, had embarrassed himself in Tokyo seven years earlier: he and his family were detained for trying to get into Japan on fake passports, supposedly to visit Tokyo Disneyland. As for Kim Jong Chul, the Dear Leader had once declared that he "resembles a girl"—hardly an asset in male-dominated North Korea.

That left only one choice. As it happened, as he moved into his late 20s, Kim Jong Un developed a striking resemblance to his grandfather Kim Il Sung. In a society mesmerized by personality cults, "that meant a lot," says North Korean defector Lee Sung Bak, once a government bureaucrat. On Sept. 27, 2010, Kim Jong Un—at 27—was named a four-star general in the Korean People's Army and appointed vice chairman of the Central Military Commission, making him second in command of the country's most powerful institution. Kim Jong Un's ascension was smooth: today everyone in a position of power in North Korea is at least twice his age and vastly more experienced, but

## Kim Jong Un became a Chicago Bulls fan when Michael Jordan was dominating the NBA

**Meet the new boss** *Visiting a Pyongyang amusement park, Kim Jong Un and wife Ri Sol Ju work the crowd in July 2012*

KOREAN CENTRAL NEWS AGENCY—AP

they will nonetheless snap off crisp salutes to him.

Two issues are critical for North Korea. Will it liberalize its economy, as its chief patron China did 30 years ago, and finally allow its citizens to get at least a whiff of the prosperity that surrounds them in East Asia? And will it give up its pariah status as a rogue nuclear state—a choice the U.S. and other governments practically begged Kim Jong Il to make, to no avail?

His schooling in Switzerland and love of basketball suggest that Kim Jong Un has tasted deeply of the forbidden fruit of the West. Already there are signs that he is allowing the impassive mask of earlier leaders to slip a bit. Smiling and waving, he has visited amuse-ment parks and attended concerts—and the world was stunned when Kim was accompanied on these public outings by an elegant partner, who was soon revealed to be his wife, referred to as Comrade Ri Sol Ju. She is believed to be from an upper-class family; her father is said to be a professor and her mother an obstetrician, according to Cheong Seong Chang. The couple may even have a child together, born in 2009. Whether that child comes of age in a repressive, isolated society or one that seeks prosperity and a wider embrace of the outside world depends in large part on his father's decisions in the years to come. ■

—By Bill Powell

**Aground** *As the ship lists to starboard, lifeboats take passengers ashore*

# Abandon Ship!

Thirty-two passengers perish when the luxury liner *Costa Concordia* runs aground off Italy's coast

**A**S 2012 BEGAN, WRITERS, PUBLISHERS, TV and movie studio executives were anticipating the fuss that would surround the centennial anniversary of the sinking of the legendary ocean liner *Titanic* on April 12. James Cameron's blockbuster 1999 film was scheduled to be rereleased in an updated 3-D format, bookstores were featuring a clutch of new volumes devoted to the famed luxury liner's demise, and TV editors were putting the final touches on a wide array of new programs devoted to *Titanic.*

Amid the fuss, no one was expecting that a modern-day ocean liner might find itself listing heavily on its side and dispatching lifeboats into the night. But that's exactly what happened when the massive Italian cruise ship *Costa Concordia* ran aground on Friday, Jan. 13, off the shore of Giglio Island in the Tyrrhenian Sea along Italy's northwest coast. The luxury liner, owned by Costa Crociere, a unit of Carnival Corp., was on a weeklong cruise of the western Mediterranean, idling along the scenic coast

about 9:45 p.m. The late-dinner service had just begun in the main dining room, when, as Sicilian native Alessandra Grasso, 24, told the New York *Times:* "In a moment, everything was up in the air. People, chairs, glasses, food."

The 1,017-ft. (310 m) -long ship, a floating resort with some 4,200 passengers and crew onboard, was passing between the coastline and Giglio, a popular tourist island 18 miles (29 km) offshore, rather than in the open sea on the far side of the island, as called for in its approved itinerary. It had struck a submerged reef or rock, tearing a 160-ft. (49 m) gash in its hull. In the moments that followed the collision, however, the ship's loudspeakers announced only a power outage and urged those aboard to remain calm. According to one passenger, dinner waiters told patrons to remain seated even as the ship began listing badly. Twenty minutes later, the order to abandon ship was issued, causing panic among the passengers and a stampede in the direction of the lifeboats.

Passengers described a nightmarish scene as they

**Under fire** *Captain Francesco Schettino was accused of leaving the ship before all passengers had disembarked*

LEFT: GIUSEPPE MODESTI—AP; RIGHT, TOP: MEDIASET—AP; BOTTOM LEFT: NICK CORNISH—REX FEATURES/AP; RIGHT: GREGORIO BORGIA—AP

swarmed, crawled and slid through the listing ship's corridors, trying to reach safety. Some threw themselves into the sea, whose waters were a frigid 57°F (14°C), and swam their way to shore, a distance of about 400 ft. (122 m). Others clambered down ladders into lifeboats, only to discover that the crew members in charge of the emergency craft were untrained and inept. "The pilots were not sailors but waiters who had no idea how to maneuver and kept on having us turning in circles," reported Giancarlo Sammatrice, 22, a vacationing cook from Sicily.

Amid the chaos, Captain Francesco Schettino, 52, abandoned ship in a lifeboat well before all passengers were accounted for. Within days, Italian newspapers published transcripts of a phone conversation between Schettino and an angry Livorno Port Authority chief Gregorio De Falco, who berated the captain and ordered him to return to the ship and determine the status of the passengers. Schettino reluctantly agreed to do so, but apparently never did. He was questioned by local police, then detained and finally put under house arrest.

Cruise line executives initially defended the crew, but they soon reversed course and implicated the captain. "I can't deny there was human error," said Costa Crociere CEO Pier Luigi Foschi. "We're talking about an initiative that commander Schettino took, according to his own will and contrary to our rules of conduct." The widespread assumption was that Schettino had ordered the ship on the unplanned course to give tourists and islanders on Giglio a close encounter with the enormous *Costa Concordia*. In a word, he may simply have been showboating.

As rescue workers scoured the ship for survivors, divers blew holes in its hull to afford access to submerged areas. Thirty-two passengers died, and at least 64 more were injured. The ship, built for more than $570 million, was declared a total loss; salvage and demolition expenses may cost more than $300 million. Fortunately, recovery efforts ensured that its fuel reserves did not leak into the sea.

Captain Schettino's fate was uncertain as this book went to press: he is accused of manslaughter, causing the shipwreck and abandoning ship before all passengers were evacuated, but authorities had yet to decide whether he or several others under investigation would stand trial. Court-appointed experts blamed Schettino for the disaster but also faulted the crew and the ship's owner for contributing to the accident, a finding that Costa Crociere denied. Unfortunately for Captain Schettino, if he does stand trial, there will be no lifeboats in the courtroom. ∎

**Rescue efforts** *At left, divers attempt to enter the capsized ship and locate passengers still trapped inside. At right, a police officer holds a baby rescued from the ship as a ferry carrying passengers reaches nearby Porto Santo Stefano on Jan. 14*

TOP: JOHN MACDOUGALL—AFP/GETTY IMAGES; BOTTOM: DAVID MOIR—REUTERS

**BRITAIN**

# Jubilee!

## Loyal subjects cheer a popular Queen on her 60-year reign

**S**HE HAS PRESIDED OVER BRITAIN FOR SIX decades now, and current Prime Minister David Cameron is the 12th PM to serve under her; the first was Winston Churchill. She has sat for roughly 200 official portraits; she has conducted more than 200 official overseas visits; and as of 2012, she is the second longest reigning monarch in British history, three years shy of Queen Victoria. So ... doesn't Queen Elizabeth II, now 86, deserve a party? Of course she does, and with the royal family enjoying a surge in popularity, Britons celebrated the Queen's Diamond Jubilee in true English fashion: with a dazzling regatta—on a foggy, rainy day. ∎

**Jolly good** *At top, Union Jacks were popular accessories as crowds cheered the Queen outside Buckingham Palace. Above, an outdoor concert ended with Prince Charles offering three cheers and a kiss of his mother's hand*

TOP: STEFAN WERMUTH—REUTERS; BOTTOM: DARREN STAPLES—WPA POOL/GETTY IMAGES

**Floating festivities** *Jubilee celebrations peaked on the first weekend of June with a royal regatta in which more than 1,000 nautical craft—including boats used in the evacuation of Dunkirk in World War II—sailed down the Thames on a moist Sunday. Leading the marine parade was a new royal barge, the* Gloriana, *center. Below, members of the royal family take in the show: from left, Kate Middleton, a.k.a. Catherine, Duchess of Cambridge; Prince Philip; Camilla, Duchess of Cornwall, and her husband Prince Charles; Queen Elizabeth II; the Queen's grandsons, Princes William and Harry*

# In Brief

## A Debt Crisis Frays Europe's Union

**ATHENS** In the photograph above, a young Greek woman confronts Athens police spattered by paint thrown by demonstrators. Tens of thousands of protesters massed in the streets of the capital on Oct. 9 to express their disapproval as German Chancellor Angela Merkel visited Greece for talks with P.M. Antonis Samaras. Some demonstrators brandished swastikas during the protests, which were only one manifestation of a year's worth of anxiety and confrontation as the nations of the European Union (E.U.) continued to suffer the effects of a sovereign debt crisis that found Greece, Spain, Italy and other indebted nations struggling to meet tough austerity measures championed by Merkel and others. In Greece, unemployment was running near 25% in 2012, while economic output shrank 20%.

German banks hold much of the debt that plagues the eurozone, and they strongly supported the austerity programs, which raised taxes and reduced government services and safety-net programs in the debtor nations. On Sept. 6, the European Central Bank announced it would launch a program to buy the government bonds of fiscally challenged nations, hoping to help alleviate the immediate burden on debtor countries. But the future of the Union and of its common currency, the euro, remained far from secure, as opinion polls continued to show dwindling support for the E.U. across the Continent.

On Oct. 12, three days after the fracas in Athens, the E.U. received good news from an unexpected quarter, when Nobel judges in Scandinavia announced that the 27-nation coalition was the winner of the 2012 Nobel Peace Prize. The peace prize judges, all of whom are Norwegians, focused on the confederation's role in preserving peace throughout a Continent long plagued by war, while admitting that the E.U. "is currently undergoing grave economic difficulties and considerable social unrest." Critics mocked the choice as coming at an utterly inappropriate moment.

## France Chooses a New Leader, and a Familiar Face Wins in Venezuela

French voters turned left, rejecting the policies of controversial President Nicolas Sarkozy, while Venezuelan voters remained on the left, keeping firebrand Hugo Chávez in office.

### Hugo Chávez: Six More Years

On Oct. 7, President Hugo Chávez of Venezuela was re-elected, for the third time, to a six-year term, outpolling challenger Henrique Capriles Radonski by 1.5 million votes, 11% of the ballots cast. But the strong foe of U.S. policies may not serve out his term: he suffers from cancer, and the state of his health is a closely guarded secret. Critics charged that Chávez

used intimidating tactics and spent many petrodollars to win victory, but the outspoken leader remains very popular with poorer Venezuelans.

### Hollande Ousts Sarkozy

After a five-year term dogged by controversy over both his policies and his imperious personal demeanor, conservative French President Nicolas Sarkozy was defeated for re-election on May 6 by Socialist Party leader François Hollande, below. The new President ran on a platform that opposed German Chancellor Angela Merkel's austerity program for the European Union and advocated using government stimulus packages to jump-start France's lagging economy.

CLOCKWISE FROM TOP LEFT: YANNIS BEHRAKIS—REUTERS; JORGE SILVA—REUTERS; LAURENT CIPRIANI—AP

## After Punk Rockers Protest, President Putin Pounces

**MOSCOW** *On Feb. 21, women members of the political activist group Pussy Riot walked into the Cathedral of Christ the Saviour in Moscow, Russian Orthodoxy's holiest site, pulled colorful balaclavas over their heads and performed a "punk prayer" on the altar: it was titled "Mother of God, Chase Putin Away!" Within minutes, guards ejected the women. Only weeks before, Vladimir Putin, campaigning to be Russia's President for a third term, had visited a monastery and denounced church-state separation. Shortly after Putin won the election, three of the women—Nadezhda Tolokonnikova, Maria Alyokhina and Yekaterina Samutsevich—were arrested for "hooliganism motivated by religious hatred." After an old-fashioned show trial, on Aug. 17, the women were found guilty and sentenced to two years in prison. In October, Samutsevich's sentence was suspended; she had arrived at the cathedral too late to participate in the event. The trial was followed around the world, as supporters expressed their solidarity with the women's cause.*

CLOCKWISE FROM TOP: SERGEY PONOMAREV—AP; DON EMMERT—AFP/GETTY IMAGES; AMIR QURESHI—AFP/GETTY IMAGES

## Targeted by the Taliban

**PAKISTAN** Fourteen-year-old activist and blogger Malala Yousafzai was shot in the head on her way home from school in the Swat Valley on Oct. 9 after Taliban assailants opened fire on her vehicle in the town of Mingora. A Taliban spokesman said she was targeted for her "secularism."

The Pakistani government had presented the precocious teenager with a National Peace Award in December 2011 for her bravery in exposing the difficulties of living in the oppressive shadow of the Taliban; the group had shuttered her prior girls' school in 2009. Yousafzai survived surgery and was flown to London, even as anti-Taliban marches were held across Pakistan, above.

**NUMBERS**

# 1.5
## MILLION

*Number of citizens who paraded in Barcelona on Sept. 11, 2012, to urge independence from Spain for Catalonia. The annual parade had never drawn more than 50,000 marchers*

# 80

*Estimated number of mummies discovered in a burial chamber at an ancient pre-Columbian complex of ruins along the coast of Peru in May 2012*

## Red Lines and Hard Lines

**ISRAEL** Relations between Israel and the U.S. were strained throughout the year, as hard-line Israeli P.M. Benjamin Netanyahu was at loggerheads with U.S. President Barack Obama over the longtime allies' strategy toward a bellicose Iran.

Netanyahu called for a "red line" approach, in which Israel, with U.S. consent, would bomb any Iranian facilities that appeared close to making a nuclear bomb. Obama's Administration advocated the continued use of tough sanctions to force Iran to the bargaining table. Below, Netanyahu took his argument to the U.N. General Assembly in September, using a chart for illustration.

# Life

FROM LEFT: NASA—JPL/CALTECH; MASHID MOHADJERIN—THE NEW YORK TIMES/REDUX; REX FEATURES/AP

> "I never expected this to happen in my lifetime."
> —Theoretical physicist Peter Higgs, who predicted the existence of the Higgs boson in 1964

**PROBING NATURE'S WAYS**

*Left: The Curiosity rover, shown in a NASA illustration, landed on the surface of Mars on Aug. 5.*

*Center: Kansas farmers David and Arlan Stackley inspect a corn crop ravaged by drought in July.*

*Right: The Large Hadron Collider in Switzerland helped locate what physicists believe may be the long-sought Higgs boson particle.*

# Wheels Down on The Red Planet

Breezing through "seven minutes of terror," NASA's Curiosity rover achieves its rendezvous with Mars

**S**OMETIMES THE WILDEST IDEAS WORK BEST. For proof, look to Mars, where NASA's latest Mars lander transformed an engineering team's high-risk brainstorming into reality on the night of Aug. 5-6, safely lowering the 1-ton, $2.5 billion Curiosity rover into Mars' Gale Crater while reminding us to think twice before laughing off the quirky spaceships in old science-fiction movies. "This rocked!" a grinning Richard Cook, the Mars Exploration Program's deputy project manager, told an auditorium filled with exuberant colleagues at the Jet Propulsion Laboratory (JPL) in Pasadena, Calif. "Seriously, wasn't that cool?"

It *was* cool, because Curiosity—a car-size mobile laboratory that's bigger and more advanced than any of its predecessors—finished its 104 million-mile (167 million-km) journey with a landing as dramatic as it was improbable. The touchdown required an extraordinary sequence of events designed to slow the incoming spacecraft from a blistering 13,000 m.p.h. to 2 m.p.h. in just seven minutes. Among the new tools in play: a 51-ft.- (15.5 m-)diameter parachute with eight suspension lines—the biggest ever used in an extraterrestrial landing—and retrorockets designed to slow the craft almost to a hover. Then there was the little matter of the spacecraft's transforming itself into a sky crane just prior to landing and using nylon cords to lower Curiosity the final 25 ft. (7.6 m) to the ground.

As it turned out, the much hyped "seven minutes of terror" that began when the spacecraft entered the Martian atmosphere instead became seven minutes of breathless cheers. Scientists and engineers repeatedly erupted in applause as each dreaded landing event—guided entry, parachute deployment, heat-shield separation—passed by uneventfully. Then came the words that seemed to make JPL's estimated 3,000 visitors catch their breath.

"Standing by for sky crane," declared flight-dynamics engineer Al Chen, who provided commentary from the mission control room. The awaited terror finally hit; the lab fell silent. Then, after a slight pause, Chen's smooth voice returned. "Touchdown confirmed!" he shouted at 10:32 p.m. Pacific time (1:32 a.m. Eastern time).

The scientists and engineers, many of whom spent 10 years working on the mission, burst into cheers and even tears as the tense seven minutes gave way to 15 jubilant minutes. Their joy soon echoed across the nation. Parents and children were cheering in Chicago, where the Adler Planetarium held a late-night pajama party so families could follow the landing live. In New York City, crowds gathered in Times Square to watch on a giant screen that usually shows only ads. NASA live-streamed the event, and the traffic was so great—with up to 23 million people watching in the four hours immediately surrounding the landing—that the space agency's servers crashed.

With the theatrics done, Curiosity was set to begin a 98-week mission—one Martian year—hunting for signs that Mars offers, or once offered, a home for microbial life. Engineers risked landing the rover inside a crater rather than in a safer, wide-open flood plain for good reason: a plain is, well, plain. Instead, NASA had, for the first time, placed a rover inside a geological treasure trove.

Gale Crater is a hole next to a mountain, and as we've all known since the first time we stepped into a puddle,

**Special delivery** *This artist's conception shows the "sky crane" maneuver that allowed the Curiosity rover to land gently on Mars. After the crane lowered the rover to a soft landing, it flew away and crashed, its work complete*

NASA/JPL-CALTECH

water and water-driven sediment tend to gather in holes. There will surely be no water in the area today, but the chemical evidence of it—and perhaps even of the biology it may once have supported—should remain. The proximity of Mount Sharp, just six miles (9.7 km) away, provides a different kind of scientific target: a heap of layered sediment some two-thirds the height of Mount Everest. That could prove to be an open geological book, with millions of years' worth of Martian strata on display. NASA plans to send the probe as far as 12 miles (19 km) from the landing site, grinding up soil samples and analyzing atmospheric conditions as it makes its way up the mountain.

"We're hoping to find materials that interacted with water," said John Grotzinger, the mission's project scientist and a geologist at the California Institute of Technology. "Pathfinder and MER [the Mars Exploration rovers] did some soil composition, but this time we'll find out the actual chemicals."

Engineers say the rover should have an easier time maintaining power than its predecessors, which suffered from dust accumulating atop their solar panels. Curiosity

**Welcome to the 'hood** *This 360° view of Curiosity's landing site was one of the first images beamed back to Earth from the rover. At right is the lip of Gale Crater, within which the rover landed. At left is Mount Sharp, which the craft will explore during the course of its primary 98-week mission*

relies on a shoebox-size nuclear generator that turns heat generated by decaying plutonium into electrical power for the onboard batteries. The generator also powers the 17 cameras arrayed around Curiosity, which have the visual acuity to resolve an object the size of a golf ball 27 yd. (24.7 m) away and the resolution to capture 1-megapixel color images from multiple perspectives. The sharpest of these imagers is mounted atop the rover's vertical mast, which rises 7 ft. (2.1 m) above ground. "You could not look this thing in the eye unless you were an NBA player," said mission systems manager Mike Watkins.

Yet Curiosity is much more than a mechanical paparazzo. The instrument suite is 10 times as massive as any previous rover's, led by a robotic arm that is part spectrometer, part rock imager, part chemistry lab. Curiosity's

ABOVE: NASA/JPL-CALTECH; RIGHT: BILL INGALLS—NASA

deck harbors an interplanetary CSI lab capable of separating gases or heating powdered samples to identify organic compounds. And atop the mast, in addition to the bristle of cameras, is an instrument that can fire a million-watt laser beam at rocks up to 23 ft. (7 m) away, vaporizing them enough for an onboard spectrometer to analyze light from the pinhead-size sparks the rocks will give off, revealing their chemical composition. Shooting X rays at nearby rock samples, another task on the agenda, will excite electrons into fingerprint-like signals that identify minerals. Finally—and most tantalizingly—Curiosity will sniff the Martian sky for atmospheric methane, a telltale hint of current organic life.

"We all feel a sense of pressure to do something profound," said Grotzinger. "But even if we don't find [biological] carbon—even in the case that life was never present on Mars—it's still an opportunity to view what might have happened in Earth's past." That view from another world, made possible by the mission's unorthodox and daring landing process, promises to be sweet indeed. ■

—By Dan Cray and Jeffrey Kluger

**Touchdown** *Exuberant mission engineers at the Jet Propulsion Lab in California cheer the successful landing*

# Extreme Weather: The New Normal?

## Wildfires, drought, Isaac and the seasons of our discontent

SEVERE WEATHER VISITED DISASTERS OF biblical proportion upon Planet Earth in 2012. In the U.S., wildfires raged across the West, while record-high temperatures teamed up with the most severe drought in more than half a century to turn the nation's Midwestern breadbasket into a vast wasteland of shriveled cornstalks and dried-up creek beds. In late August, Gulf Coast residents braced for Hurricane Isaac to make landfall—seven years to the day since Hurricane Katrina flooded New Orleans and battered Gulf shores— even as unrelenting typhoon rains inundated Asia's cities.

Scientists have long predicted that extreme weather would accompany climate change. One irrefutable sign that the planet was heating up came on Sept. 16, when satellite images showed that the Arctic ice cap had receded to the lowest expanse in three decades of recording. Six weeks later, on Oct. 29, Superstorm Sandy, one of the largest storms in U.S. history, plowed ashore along an immense swath of the East Coast, devastating coastal communities, swamping New York City's streets and shutting down the great metropolis. Said New York Governor Andrew Cuomo: "Anyone who says there's not a dramatic change in weather patterns ... is denying reality ... We have a 100-year flood every two years now." ■

CLOCKWISE FROM TOP LEFT: KARI GREER—U.S. FOREST SERVICE/AP; JOHN JAVELLANA—AP; SETH PERLMAN—AP

## WILDFIRES IN THE WEST

The long, hot summer in the U.S. spawned brutal forest fires in Western states, especially Colorado, which grappled with the worst fires in its history.

An unusually warm winter in 2011-12 meant that the fire season started earlier than usual, while the lack of snowfall, especially in the mountain West, meant that dryer-than-normal forests became tinder waiting for a spark.

By late summer, a new spate of big fires began igniting in the Pacific Northwest. At left, flames of the Trinity Ridge Fire approach a barn in Featherville, Idaho, on Aug. 24; the town was ordered evacuated the week before. According to the National Interagency Fire Center, as of late September, wildfires had incinerated more than 8.5 million acres across the country.

## TYPHOON FLOODS IN ASIA

The Philippines, Taiwan and China were the primary victims of Typhoon Saola, a Category 2 hurricane that struck in late July and early August, causing more than 65 deaths and an estimated $38 million in damages. The Philippines was the hardest hit, as floodwaters inundated Manila, displacing up to 20,000 residents. China's Hubei province was also hammered by Saola's winds, rains and storm surges; more than 135,000 people were forced from their homes.

Above, a rescue boat is filled with evacuees in San Juan, outside Manila, on Aug. 8. Thousands of people were stranded on rooftops as the city's streets filled with floodwaters.

## MIDWEST DROUGHT

Even as the U.S. fought to recover from a deep economic recession, farmers in the Midwest were hit by the most wide-ranging and destructive drought in more than 50 years. Corn yields fell at least 16%, and prices rose to record highs as farmers confronted fields of dust and saw their ponds dry up. At left, Tony Frost of Frost Farms surveys one such pond in Tallula, Ill.; in a normal year, it would be a watering hole for 300 of his cattle.

By late August, the Mississippi River was running so low that authorities closed down shipping on an 11-mile (17.7 km) stretch of the Big Muddy outside Greenville, Miss. In early September, the remnants of Hurricane Isaac brought rain to states in the lower Midwest—but by then it was too late to save the crops.

## HURRICANE ISAAC

Residents of the Gulf Coast battened down their hatches and locked up their storm shutters as slow-moving Hurricane Isaac headed their way in late August, seven years after Hurricane Katrina memorably pounded the region. On Aug. 29, the Category 1 storm was lashing southern Louisiana, Mississippi and Alabama, with some gusts topping 100 m.p.h., and driving before it a storm surge of more than 7 ft. (2.1 m). The refortified levees of New Orleans held this time around, but an older levee in Plaquemines Parish was overtopped. More than 850,000 coast residents lost power for days; estimated damages may total more than $1 billion.

Above, Isaac's winds grafted a gazebo onto the rear end of a pickup truck amid the flooded streets of Braithwaite, La., on Sept. 1. At right, storm-surge waves pummeled Ken Combs Pier in Gulfport, Miss., on Aug. 29.

## ARCTIC SEA ICE

The state of the Arctic, already bad, may have made the dreaded jump to worse in the summer of 2012, as new images revealed that the sea ice that caps the Arctic Ocean melted to its lowest expanse since at least 1979, when satellites first began keeping track of ice over the North Pole. The National Snow and Ice Data Center reported that Arctic ice had fallen to 1.32 million sq. mi., or 24%, of the surface of the Arctic Ocean, on Sept. 16. The previous low, set in 2007, was 29%.

The NASA visualization below shows the extent of Arctic sea ice in September 2012; the yellow line shows its typical expanse between 1979-2010. TIME's Bryan Walsh wrote, "Here's the real irony: the most immediate impact of climate change–related Arctic ice melting will likely be the opening of vast new drilling territory for a thirsty oil industry."

At bottom, crew from the U.S. Coast Guard cutter *Healy,* who are studying the effects of climate change on the Arctic in the NASA-sponsored ICESCAPE mission, retrieve supplies dropped by parachute onto ice floes.

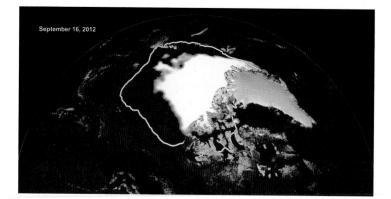

September 16, 2012

CLOCKWISE FROM TOP LEFT: MARIO TAMA—GETTY IMAGES; SCIENTIFIC VISUALIZATION STUDIO, NASA GODDARD SPACE FLIGHT CENTER; NASA/ REUTERS; TIM ISBELL—BILOXI SUN HERALD/MCT/GETTY IMAGES

# Marissa Mayer

Can an overachiever from Google help Yahoo get its yodel back?

SILICON VALLEY LIKES LEADERS WITH star power, and stars don't come any bigger than Marissa Mayer, 37, who was named to head troubled online giant Yahoo on July 16. Her résumé is surely the template for a postmodern, information-age celebrity CEO: Stanford artificial-intelligence degree, employee No. 20 at Google, developer of the iconic white search page, user-experience guru. The private life of the stunning blond is also media bait: Mayer lives in a penthouse suite atop the Four Seasons hotel in San Francisco, complete with a bespoke Dale Chihuly art-glass chandelier; prefers her pal Oscar de la Renta's designs for dress-up occasions; and hired the Killers as her wedding band.

The whip-smart computer engineer made more headlines when she declared she was pregnant the same day Yahoo hired her. But investors just wanted to know how she would help the failing company regain its vigor. Fortunately, Yahoo now has someone at the helm who shares much of the Steve Jobs worldview. Here are three reasons Mayer is a smart pick to reinvent one of the Internet's iconic brands.

**1.** She's a user-experience fanatic. Like Jobs, Mayer focuses on how consumers interact with technology— she played a big role in developing Google's search engine, location services and design aesthetic. The user experience is key, because technology is no longer an industry in which innovation is driven by business users but rather by individuals; BlackBerry inventor RIM lost huge market share to Apple when smartphones became ubiquitous. Mayer's design propensities mirror Jobs' consumer-first tendencies— she emphasizes simplicity and ease of use and has "a great eye for the look and feel of a site," said Benjamin Schachter, a tech analyst at Macquarie Securities Group in New York City.

**2.** She's a technologist who understands media, not a media person trying to get technology. In the battle between tech and media, the geeks are still winning. "Any company that has information and data at its core ought to have a techie running it," said Keith Woolcock, founder of the technology-research firm 5th Column Ideas. "We live in a media-centric world, but it's mediated by technology." Mayer's product focus will cheer investors who have grown weary of Yahoo's ill-fated efforts to define itself as a content company. And her coding chops will garner respect from the engineers; she'll need them to help pick up the pace and quality of innovation at Yahoo.

**3.** She's a woman, and technology is feminizing. Female leaders are rare in technology; they represent a mere 9.1% of Silicon Valley board members (vs. 16.1% of FORTUNE 500 board members). Yet women have become the leading users of technology—they execute more than half of all searches, spend the majority of time on most major social-media sites and use mobile devices far more than men do. They are also more likely than men to buy tablets, laptops and smartphones. Yahoo's user base is already significantly more female than Google's (51.3% vs. 42.6%). Tellingly, the best-loved technology brand among women is Apple, according to a Boston Consulting Group study, for "ease and intuitiveness of use" as well as for the company's "anti-establishment image."

Mayer believes in the former and projects the latter; she took heat in the blogosphere for saying she would work through her few weeks of maternity leave. But extreme jobs are the way of the fast-paced Valley, where 70-hour workweeks are standard. And as Mayer has said, "I like to get myself in over my head." A lucky trait for a new mom—and for a CEO hoping to lead an epic turnaround for a long-drifting company.
                                        —By Rana Foroohar

## Mayer is a technologist who understands media, not a media person trying to get technology

ROBYN TWOMEY—CORBIS OUTLINE

**Digital diva** *"This wonderful and powerful medium, the Internet, is empowering geeks—and especially female geeks—to express and pursue their passions,"* Mayer has said

# In Brief

## A Loss of Face for Facebook

**TECHNOLOGY** For Mark Zuckerberg and the company he co-founded in 2004, the past eight years have been an exhilarating ride in one direction: straight up. Facebook, nurtured in a Harvard University dorm room, has become the dominant player in online media: as of October 2012, more than 1 billion people around the world had Facebook pages, and the tale of the website's genesis was made into the Oscar-winning film *The Social Network* in 2010.

So when Zuckerberg (at microphone) rang the bell to start trading on the NASDAQ stock exchange on May 18, when Facebook shares went on sale in an initial public offering, or IPO, most observers thought the price per share would rise rapidly from the opening price of $38. Instead, it sharply fell.

From the get-go, the IPO seemed hexed: computer issues delayed trading shortly after the trading day began, and that was only the beginning of the bad news for Facebook. The stock price continued in the doldrums, and by early October, shares were trading at around $22. Investors, it seemed, were not convinced that Facebook could translate its gazillions of gazers into daily dollars—and they hit the "dislike" button.

## West Nile Virus Returns

**HEALTH** It was one of the worst years for West Nile virus since the disease first hit the U.S., in 1999. By late September, 48 states had reported cases of the disease, totaling 3,545 nationwide and 47 deaths. Eight states accounted for 70% of the cases: Texas, Mississippi, South Dakota, Michigan, California, Louisiana, Oklahoma and Illinois.

Only 20% of those infected suffered major symptoms, which include headache, fatigue and body pain. There is no specific treatment for the ailment, which begins in birds and spreads via mosquitoes.

## The Great Sandwich War

**SOCIETY** Americans often find themselves fighting cultural wars on unexpected battlegrounds, but the brouhaha that mixed up gay rights with a fast-food chain's chicken sandwiches established a new standard for outré face-offs. Georgia-based Chick-fil-A become a magnet for controversy after COO Dan Cathy declared to the *Baptist Press* in July that he was "guilty as charged" in supporting "the biblical definition of the family unit." The company's charitable foundation has lent major support to antigay organizations.

Later in July, former Arkansas governor and current TV commentator Mike Huckabee urged his followers to patronize Chick-fil-A restaurants on Aug. 1 to show their support for traditional marriage. Encouraged by such conservative icons as Sarah Palin and Rick Santorum, the proposal caught fire, and on the appointed day, Chick-fil-A restaurants in Southern and Midwestern states were swamped by the, well, filet-in.

The unusual protest drew an equal and opposite reaction from advocates of gay rights. "Kiss-ins" between same-sex couples were held at the chain's restaurants in many states, while mayors in some more liberal cities suggested that Chick-fil-A should stay away. In September the chain declared its foundation would re-evaluate its political donation process, but unconvinced critics called for action rather than words.

The battle over gay marriage will continue in more traditional arenas: the issue was on November election ballots in four states, and the U.S. Supreme Court is expected to address same-sex marriage in its 2012-13 term.

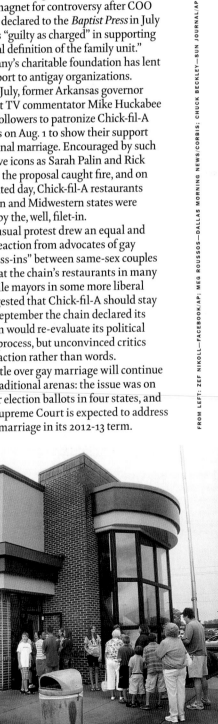

FROM LEFT: ZEF NIKOLL—FACEBOOK/AP; MEG ROUSSOS—DALLAS MORNING NEWS/CORBIS; CHUCK BECKLEY—SUN JOURNAL/AP

## A Monster Machine, a Minuscule Particle and a Major Breakthrough

**SCIENCE** *Move over, Captain Ahab. On July 4, scientists working with the Large Hadron Collider at the European Organization for Nuclear Research (CERN) said they had evidence proving the existence of a particle called the Higgs boson, the white whale of physics since it was first postulated in 1964. The particle is the reason mass exists in the universe, for energy and matter, like steam and ice, are two different states of the same thing. If you can't ping energetic particles with something, then planets, suns, galaxies, moons, comets, dogs and people would not exist. The "ping thing," we now know, is the Higgs boson. The discovery validated physicists' Standard Model, the 1970s theory that describes three great forces that drive the universe: the weak nuclear force, the strong force and electromagnetism.*

### A Dragon by the Tail

**SPACE** Even as NASA flew its remaining space shuttles into museum retirement, a new era in space travel was dawning. At 8:56 a.m. CST on May 25, NASA flight engineer Don Pettit, aboard the International Space Station (ISS), reached out with the station's maneuvering arm and grabbed hold of the 12-ft. (3.7 m) -wide, 20-ft. (6.1 m) -long Dragon capsule, the first private spacecraft successfully launched to the ISS. The feat was a triumph for the Obama Administration, which has supported the privatization of orbital research, and for Elon Musk, the wealthy Silicon Valley entrepreneur whose company, SpaceX, fathered the Dragon.

CLOCKWISE FROM TOP: REX FEATURES/AP; KAREN L. KING; REUTERS/NASA

**NUMBERS**

# $10 BILLION

*Price tag to build the Large Hadron Collider at the CERN facility in Switzerland, which was used to accelerate and smash subatomic particles and thus identify the Higgs boson*

# 2 MILLION

*Number of iPhone 5 devices sold in the new phone's first 24 hours on sale —and before problems with its Maps application emerged*

### Did Jesus Have a Spouse?

**RELIGION** Scholars and laypeople were excited by the news that a 2nd century A.D. Egyptian papyrus fragment suggests that Jesus Christ may have had a wife. In September Karen L. King, a scholar at Harvard Divinity School, said that six words written in Sahidic Coptic declare, "Jesus said to them: 'My wife ...' "

"This fragment and that sentence are not evidence of Jesus' marital status," King explained, noting that the papyrus, which came her way in 2010 from an anonymous collector, was written at a time when accounts of the life and teachings of Christ were very much in flux, and may simply reflect the viewpoint of Copts (Egyptian Christians) who were arguing against celibacy as a religious practice. Some onlookers queried the fragment's authenticity.

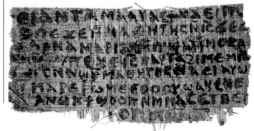

# Sports

FROM LEFT: DON EMMERT—AFP/GETTY IMAGES; FELIPE TRUEBA—EFE/ZUMA PRESS; JONATHAN FERREY—GETTY IMAGES

"I think the Games were absolutely fabulous."

—IOC President Jacques Rogge, on the London Olympics

VICTORY'S TRAJECTORY

*Left: Golf sensation Rory McIlroy, 23, of Northern Ireland, celebrates after handily winning the PGA Championship on Aug. 12.*
*Middle: Competitors in the men's 10-km swimming event dive into the Serpentine lake in Hyde Park at the London Olympics on Aug. 10.*
*Right: Dario Franchitti, 39, holds a fist*

# Britannia Rules The Games

Bolt dazzled and Phelps churned, but the real stars of the 2012 Summer Olympics were a plucky host city and a cadre of superb female athletes

**Five-ring circus** *A barge in the Thames sports illuminated Olympic rings, for those who may have missed them on the Tower Bridge at rear*

MARK KOLBE—GETTY IMAGES; CAULDRON: LEON NEAL—AFP/GETTY IMAGES (4)

**F**ASTER, HIGHER, STRONGER? NOT THIS TIME. To hear a chorus of global naysayers before the London Summer Games of 2012 opened on July 27, the motto of these Olympics might have been Scarier, Messier, Darker. Terrorist attacks were likely, the authorities were ill-prepared amateurs, ordinary Britons despised

**MICHAEL PHELPS**
The U.S. star of the Beijing Games, 27, didn't even medal in his first race, the 400-m individual medley; Ryan Lochte took the gold. Then Phelps caught fire, winning six more medals. With 22 career medals—18 of them gold—he is the most decorated Olympian in history.

**U.S. WOMEN'S GYMNASTICS TEAM**
America's "Fierce Five"—from left, McKayla Maroney, Jordyn Wieber, Gabby Douglas, Aly Raisman and Kyla Ross—won gold in the team competition, with Russia and Romania placing second and third.

the thought of the Games, and an overcrowded London would be either paralyzed or chaotic—take your pick.

But by the time film director Danny Boyle's extravagant opening ceremonies ended—after William Blake's "green and pleasant land" as well as his "dark satanic mills" had been re-created inside the main Olympic Stadium, after James Bond and Queen Elizabeth II (or a stand-in) had parachuted onto the field, after studly David Beckham had roared up the Thames in a motorboat to deliver the Olympic torch in unforgettable fashion—the London fog of negativity that had long surrounded the Games began to dispel, and even the stiffest of upper lips began to relax

into a smile. With each passing day, as the athletes displayed their skills, the Games became more compelling and rewarding. By the time London's raffish Mayor Boris Johnson passed along the Olympic flag to Rio de Janeiro's Mayor, Eduardo Paes, on Aug. 12, there was no doubt that the 2012 Summer Games had been a roaring success.

A fascinating storyline emerged early on: these were the first Olympics to be dominated by women athletes. The U.S. fielded its first female-majority team: women outnumbered men, 268 to 261, and they won more medals than did the U.S. men. Women also made up the majority on the Russian and Chinese squads. In London the

TOP: FRANCOIS XAVIER MARIT—AFP/GETTY IMAGES; BOTTOM: RONALD MARTINEZ—GETTY IMAGES

TOP: BILL FRAKES—SPORTS ILLUSTRATED/GETTY IMAGES; BOTTOM: FRISO GENTSCH—DPA/CORBIS

**USAIN BOLT**

Four years after dazzling the world in Beijing, Jamaica's sensational sprinter defended his 2008 gold medals in both the 100-m and 200-m races, setting a new Olympic record of 9.63 sec. in the former event. The Napoleon of the track then crowned himself as a "legend" at 26—and few voices argued.

**SANYA RICHARDS-ROSS**

Competing in her third Olympics, the 27-year-old U.S. speedster won gold in the 400-m event and in the 4 x 400 m relay. U.S. runner Allyson Felix, 26, won three golds, in the 200-m, 4 x 100-m and 4 x 400-m events, as Americans dominated the oval.

full diversity of the world's women was on display, from the barely-there bikinis of the beach volleyball competitors to the black head covering that a 16-year-old Saudi, Wojdan Shaherkani, wore to compete in judo.

On Aug. 4, Jessica Ennis, Britain's luminous heptathlete, put a charge into Olympic Stadium as she blazed down the straightaway to claim the 800-m event—and the gold—before a delirious crowd. And all eyes turned to the soccer pitch on Aug. 6, when the U.S. women's soccer team clashed with their Canadian cousins in an epic and thrilling semifinal, winning 4-3 in the dying seconds of overtime. (The U.S. men's team failed to even qualify for the Games.) The U.S. women went on to defeat Japan 2-1 in the gold medal match.

The joyous parade of amazons marched on, propelling the entire Games. In gymnastics, American Gabby Douglas achieved a pioneering twofer, becoming the first African American to win the coveted all-around title and the first U.S. gymnast to flip and tumble her way to gold in both that event and the team competition. In the first Games to feature female boxing, Irish slugger Katie Taylor became an overnight hero to her countrymen, while a speedy U.S. women's team turned the individual and relay track events into a London Gold Rush.

Yet if the women's ascendance was riveting, their male counterparts also dazzled. The single athlete who towered over the Games was Jamaican sprinter Usain Bolt, 26, who scampered to first place in both the 100-m and 200-m dashes. The 6-ft. 5-in. (195-cm.) superman celebrated in memorable fashion, proving he is not only the planet's fastest person but also its reigning showman. Holding his finger to his lips during his 200-m victory, he shushed his critics; he also performed push-ups, struck his familiar "archer" pose and engaged in rampant PDAs with the Jamaican flag. Had a rhythmic gymnast appeared with a hoop, Bolt would no doubt have jumped through it.

Like Bolt, American Michael Phelps was a hero of the 2008 Beijing Games who seemed not to have aged in four years. After a slow start, Phelps and his rival-cum-teammate, Ryan Lochte, put on a terrific show as they dueled each other in individual events and trounced all comers in the team relays. As the closing ceremonies ended, Phelps stood alone as the most decorated athlete in Olympic history—and London 2012 stood tall as one of the most memorable, civil and thrilling Games in recent memory. Or, to put it in official Olympics lingo: Memorabler, Civiler, Thrillinger. ■

**U.S. WOMEN'S BEACH VOLLEYBALL TEAM**
The familiar U.S. duo of Kerri Walsh Jennings, 34, in sunglasses, and partner Misty May-Traenor, 35, claimed their third Olympic gold medal in London. Close friends off the court, the two women have been global ambassadors for their increasingly popular sport.

**U.S. WOMEN'S SOCCER TEAM**
Midfielder Carli Lloyd (No. 10) of the U.S. goes up for a header against Yuki Ogimi, 25, of Japan in the final match. Lloyd, 30, scored both U.S. goals as the Americans won, 2-1, making up for the team's surprising loss to Japan in the 2011 World Cup.

**U.S. MEN'S BASKETBALL TEAM**
Shushing his vocal doubters, Usain Bolt–style, LeBron James, 27, led a scrappy, undersized U.S. team to the gold medal over Spain. Only a few weeks before, James and the Miami Heat had beaten the Oklahoma City Thunder to win the NBA title.

RIGHT PAGE, FROM LEFT: BEN STANSALL—AFP/GETTY IMAGES; JAMIE SQUIRE—GETTY IMAGES; HARRY E. WALKER—MCT/ZUMAPRESS

LEFT: JASON O'BRIEN—ACTION IMAGES/ZUMAPRESS; RIGHT: MICHAEL STEELE—GETTY IMAGES

### OSCAR PISTORIUS

South Africa's intrepid "Blade Runner," left, was one of the heroes of the Games, as he became the first amputee athlete to compete in the Olympics. Though he did not qualify for the finals in his strongest event, the 400-m run, Pistorius, 25, competed in the 4 x 400-m relay final as a member of South Africa's team.

### MO FARAH

He was born in Somalia and he trains in the U.S., but Mohammed (Mo) Farah, 29, competes for Britain, where he became a national hero after claiming the gold medal in both the 10,000-m and 5,000-m races. Farah's running coach in Oregon is the legendary marathon champion Alberto Salazar.

**GABBY DOUGLAS**
**U.S. | Gymnastics**

**RYAN LOCHTE**
**U.S. | Swimming**

**OLYMPICS 2012**

# Faces of The Games

**KATIE TAYLOR**
**Ireland | Boxing**

**PRINCE WILLIAM AND KATE MIDDLETON**
**Britain | Royals**

LEFT PAGE, CLOCKWISE FROM TOP LEFT: RONALD MARTINEZ—GETTY IMAGES; ROBERT BECK—SPORTS ILLUSTRATED/GETTY IMAGES; SCOTT HEAVEY—GETTY IMAGES; I-IMAGES/ZUMAPRESS. RIGHT PAGE, CLOCKWISE FROM TOP LEFT: LEON NEAL—AFP/GETTY IMAGES; IMAGO/ZUMAPRESS; STANLEY CHOU—GETTY IMAGES; THOMAS COEX—AFP/GETTY IMAGES; ADAM PRETTY—GETTY IMAGES; MIKE HEWITT—GETTY IMAGES

**ANDY MURRAY**
**Britain | Tennis**

**FATIMA SULAIMAN DAHMAN**
**Yemen | Track**

**DAVID RUDISHA**
**Kenya | Track**

**HOPE SOLO**
**U.S. | Soccer**

**MISSY FRANKLIN**
**U.S. | Swimming**

**McKALA MARONEY**
**U.S. | Gymnastics**

# Bubba Watson

His swing defies golf's rules—and maybe Newton's laws of motion

**B**UBBA WATSON HAS THREE FEARS IN LIFE: darkness, heights and crowds. The first two won't hurt you in golf. But the third seems pretty problematic because in 2012 the Floridian, 33, became the Masters champ and golf's reigning stuntman, and his galleries will only grow.

Watson is the most inventive player in golf. He has to be, since his majestic drives often veer off course. That's when the magic show starts. He thrives on hooking and slicing the ball around any tree, bunker or water hazard. Note his miracle on the second play-off hole at the Masters: he forced a ball to fly out of the Augusta, Ga., woods, make a 40-yd. (35-m) right turn and fall within 10 ft. (3 m) of the cup, clinching the green jacket. "I want to try a shot that nobody can pull off," he says. "Or just amaze people. That's the thrill."

Golf is loaded with swing technicians and books on how to play the game. Yet Watson has never taken a golf lesson or hired a personal coach. His swing breaks nearly every rule. His feet shuffle, his hips turn too violently, his arc is wild. But his gyrations create tremendous club speed and power. On average, his drives travel 315 yds., the longest on the PGA Tour.

Watson's emotional reaction to his Masters win—he couldn't stop crying—also won fans over. He was thinking of his father Gerry, a Vietnam vet who mentored him on public courses and died of throat cancer in 2010. And he was thinking of his son. Five days before he left for the Masters, Watson and his wife Angie picked up a month-old baby named Caleb, whom they had just adopted after a four-year process that had been an ordeal.

The left-hander's recent ascent was a surprise, given that his career nearly imploded a few years ago, when he was playing poorly and throwing public temper tantrums. A Tour player since 2006, he had 120 starts but no wins as of 2010, when his caddie, Ted Scott, sat him down and delivered an ultimatum: Tone it down, or I'll quit. Watson embraced the critique, controlled his emotions and won his first PGA tournament three weeks later. Now, two years on from that first championship, Watson's game is coming together, both on and off the course. That's the thrill, and he'll just have to learn to live with the crowds it attracts. ∎

—*By Sean Gregory*

VISIONHAUS/CORBIS

# Jeremy Lin

## Linsanity! An acrobatic point guard makes NBA hoops fun again

HONEST BASKETBALL FANS WILL TELL you the truth: the NBA's regular season is basically a series of exhibition contests, as the game's top stars save their energy for the long playoff series that lead to the finals. But not in February 2012, when the sudden rise of New York Knicks point guard Jeremy Lin, 24, from benchwarmer to superstar crushed all kinds of conventions—like the one that said he was a nice Ivy League player but would never thrive in the NBA. How many Harvard grads and how many Asian Americans were in the current NBA before Lin arrived? Zero and zero. Harvard has produced more U.S. Presidents (eight) than NBA players (four, and until Lin, none since the 1950s).

Lin's bottom-feeding Knicks began the lockout-shortened 2011-12 season in chaos. After the desperate head coach, Mike D'Antoni, finally gave the ball to Lin, all Lin did was go out and score more points in his first five starts—136—than any other player since the NBA-ABA merger in 1976. And it wasn't just the scoring, it was the head-turning way Lin scored: seemingly from everywhere on the court and with giddy flair, playing the elusive Road Runner and making the game's best defenders look like Wiley Coyote. And when he wasn't scoring, Lin was making magnificent no-look passes that sent fans into delirium.

The overnight phenom was raised in Palo Alto, Calif., where his father Gie-Ming Lin, a computer engineer, studied film of Larry Bird, Kareem Abdul-Jabbar and other NBA stars and tutored young Jeremy at the local YMCA—after his son finished his homework. Indeed, Lin fought Asian-American stereotypes as his game improved. When he entered the gym for one summer-league game, someone redirected him: no one was playing volleyball that night. Lin led his high school team to a state championship, and despite a strong senior year at Harvard, no NBA team picked Lin in the draft. He persevered, though, and ended up on the Knicks' bench after unimpressive stints with the Golden State Warriors and Houston Rockets.

Lin was smart, articulate, charming and humble. He was also a devout Christian, and when his talents were seemingly born again early in 2012, the frenzy over his playing circled the globe. His No. 17 jersey became the top online seller in the NBA, while the league's TV partners in China, Taiwan and the Philippines rushed to add Knicks games. Soon the media in China and Taiwan were caught up in *Linfengkuang*—Linsanity.

Sadly, Linsanity—and Lin—came down to earth at last; a knee injury ended his season early, after which he became a restricted free agent and signed a three-year, $25 million contract with his old team, the Rockets. Yet legions of fans will always recall that one brief shining moment that was known as *Linfengkuang*. ■

BILL KOSTROUN—AP

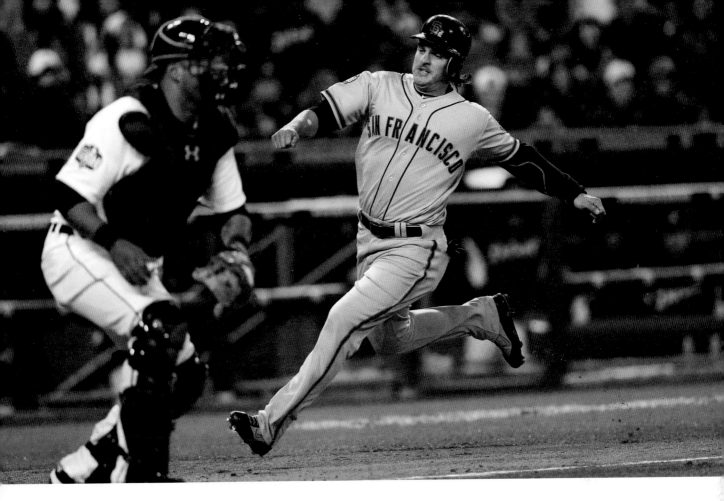

TOP: DOUG PENSINGER—GETTY IMAGES. BOTTOM: JUERGEN HASENKOPF—REX FEATURES/AP;

SPORTS

# Contenders. Out with the old: young stars excelled in 2012

### ANDY MURRAY

For years now, Scottish tennis ace Andy Murray, left, has been hoping to join the top stars of the men's game. But Murray, 25, had been beaten in the final round of four majors. In 2012 he lost to Roger Federer at Wimbledon in July. But in August, Murray caught fire, beating Federer to win gold at the London Olympics, then topping Novak Djokovic to win the U.S. Open in September.

### MIAMI HEAT

The Miami Heat, right, had failed to meet expectations since controversial star LeBron James joined the team in 2010. In the strike-shortened 2012 season, James silenced his critics, leading the Heat to victory over a surprising Oklahoma City Thunder squad in the NBA finals. The star forward (with tongue out) was named MVP of the series.

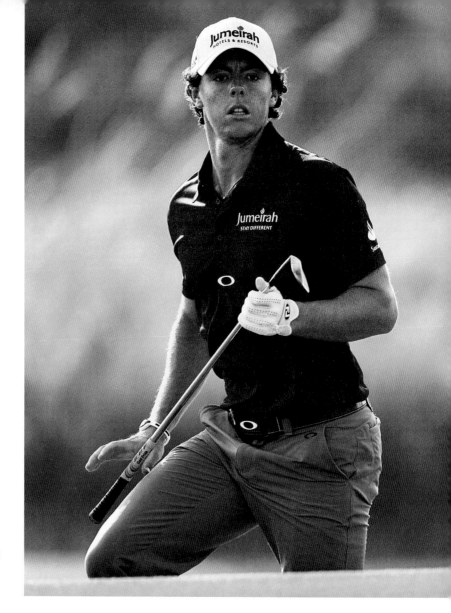

### SAN FRANCISCO GIANTS

Ryan Theriot, 32, races home with the winning run in the 10th inning of Game 4 of the World Series, left, as the colorful Giants, riding a hot streak, swept the Detroit Tigers in the Series, 4-0. Tigers sluggers Prince Fielder, 28, and Miguel Cabrera, 29—who became baseball's first Triple Crown winner since 1967—couldn't get their bats going against the Giants' formidable pitchers and sterling defense.

If the Series lacked sizzle, the playoffs were thrilling, as the St. Louis Cardinals just kept winning until they ran into the streaking Giants, and Detroit swept the punchless, aging New York Yankees to get to the fall classic.

### RORY MCILROY

Northern Ireland's golf phenom first made headlines in 2011, when he won the U.S. Open by eight strokes at only 22. In 2012 fan favorite McIlroy started slowly, but he won the PGA Tournament at Kiawah Island in South Carolina, right, as well as three other tourneys, took over the rank of No. 1 in the world and led the PGA in earnings. The best golfer on the planet turned a venerable 23 in May.

TOP: CHUCK BURTON—AP; BOTTOM: JOE MURPHY—NBAE/GETTY IMAGES

## I'LL HAVE ANOTHER

With each passing year, horse racing's Triple Crown seems to become a more elusive goal: it has now been 34 years since Affirmed swept the Kentucky Derby, the Preakness Stakes and the Belmont Stakes. In 2012, the gutsy Thoroughbred I'll Have Another, above, made a run for the crown, winning the first two races. But the chestnut stallion was scratched from the Belmont Stakes the day before the race due to tendinitis. I'll Have Another retired, and Union Rags won the Belmont.

## SERENA WILLIAMS

She has had her ups and downs over the years, but as the photo at left amply demonstrates, Serena Williams, now 31, enjoyed a buoyant comeback in 2012. Plagued by injuries in 2010-11, Williams started slowly in 2012, but she reached full cruising speed when she handily beat Agnieszka Radwanska at Wimbledon, left. She went on to defeat Maria Sharapova to win the gold medal at the London Olympics and to beat Victoria Azarenka in the U.S. Open.

TOP: ECLIPSE SPORTSWIRE—ZUMA PRESS/CORBIS; BOTTOM: EXPRESS NEWSPAPERS—AP

# Contours. New buildings dazzle the eye with shape-shifting magic

### HEYDAR ALIYEV CULTURAL CENTER

Iraqi-British architect Zaha Hadid's cultural center in Azerbaijan's capital, Baku, seems to echo the wind-shaped dunes of the arid nation's desert spaces. Discussing her style, the architect told TIME in 2012, "it started off through figuring out what to do with lightness or flight. Later it had to do more with topography and landscape, emulating a natural form." Folds within the building's single, undulating roof highlight the center's component parts.

### PHOENIX INTERNATIONAL MEDIA CENTER

Shown under construction, this torus-shaped headquarters for a Beijing new-media company is composed of three sections. Two large office buildings, one 10 stories high, are nestled within the outer glass façade of the complex. The architects are the Beijing firm BIAD UFo.

LEFT, FROM TOP: FARUD KHAYRULIN; DIEGO AZUBEL—EPA/CORBIS. RIGHT: ASHOK SAXENA—DEMOTIX/CORBIS

"It's way cool that he's a fan. It speaks to the relevancy of the show. It's hugely validating." —Claire Danes, on *Homeland* watcher Barack Obama

SINGULAR SENSATIONS

*Left: Claire Danes won an Emmy for her performance in the tense drama of domestic terrorism,* Homeland.

*Center: The new Barnes Foundation museum building in Philadelphia was designed by architects Tod Williams and Billie Tsien.*

*Right: The Museum of Modern Art in New York City offered a career retrospective of photographer (and subject) Cindy Sherman.*

# The Culture

FROM LEFT: RONEN AKERMAN—SHOWTIME; FLOTO + WARNER; RICHARD PERRY—THE NEW YORK TIMES/REDUX

TOP: RON BIJLSMA—NEWSPORT/ZUMA PRESS/CORBIS; BOTTOM: ROSE PALMISANO—ZUMA PRESS/CORBIS

## DARIO FRANCHITTI

The Scotsman with the Italian name, right, is emerging as one of auto racing's all-time greats. On May 27, 2012, as Takuma Sato challenged him for first place on the last lap, Franchitti, 39, slipped by to win the Indianapolis 500 as Sato lost control; it was the driver's third victory at the Brickyard. Married to Hollywood star Ashley Judd, Franchitti is also a four-time winner of the IndyCar racing series.

## LA KINGS

Based in sunny Los Angeles, the lowly LA Kings had played in the NHL finals only once in their 45-year history, losing to Montreal in 1993. Not in 2012: seeded eighth in the divisional playoffs, the Kings surged into the finals and beat the New Jersey Devils in six games to win the Stanley Cup. But the opening of the 2012-13 season was significantly delayed by labor woes, even as the NHL was enjoying an overdue rejuvenation.

## THE SHARD

Soaring above the Tower Bridge near its base, the London Bridge Tower—more commonly called the Shard, or the Shard of Glass—became the tallest building in Europe when it opened on July 5, 2012. Architect Renzo Piano designed the structure, which roughly takes the form of a pyramid coated with, yes, shards of glass.

The Shard is home to offices, a hotel, a restaurant, 10 apartments and a viewing platform. It ascends to 1,016 ft. (310 m), but its reign as Europe's tallest will be short: a skyscraper in Moscow due to open before 2013 will top out at 73 ft. (22 m) higher. The Shard's 11,000 panes of glass are each set inclining slightly inward to create a lofty mosaic of ever changing reflections of the sky.

# Characters. Familiar stars tackled challenging new roles in 2012

### KEIRA KNIGHTLEY AS ANNA KARENINA

After idling adrift in the horse latitudes in the *Pirates of the Caribbean* series, Knightley, 27, had to stretch to play the famed, flawed heroine of Leo Tolstoy's classic novel. Audiences lavished praise on the sumptuous décor of director Joe Wright's film, but critic Chris Tookey of Britain's *Daily Mail* declared, "Exquisite to look upon but fatally low in feeling."

### MATTHEW MCCONAUGHEY AS DALLAS

Time was when McConaughey seemed to play the same vacuous hunk in every film. But in 2012, amid an ongoing mid-career makeover that has seen him playing darker, more offbeat roles, the actor, 42, shone as Dallas in the witty girls'-night-out satire *Magic Mike*. O.K., his male stripper was a hunk—but a hunk who was in on the joke.

### ZOE KAZAN AS RUBY SPARKS

Actress and screenwriter Kazan, 29, wrote herself a great role as a novelist's imaginary muse who becomes real in *Ruby Sparks*. But the indie Pygmalion story didn't strike sparks with TIME's Richard Corliss: "*Ruby Sparks* tries its damnedest to make a picture that seduces moviegoers into accepting it as their best imaginary friend forever. But the sweat shows more than the sparkle."

CLOCKWISE FROM TOP: LAURIE SPARHAM—FOCUS FEATURES; GLEN WILSON—WARNER BROTHERS; MERRICK MORTON—FOX SEARCHLIGHT/EVERETT COLLECTION

### DANIEL DAY-LEWIS AS ABRAHAM LINCOLN

His indelible turns as disabled Irishman Christy Brown in *My Left Foot*, James Fenimore Cooper's Natty Bumppo in *The Last of the Mohicans* and Bill the Butcher in *Gangs of New York* revealed Day-Lewis to be one of the screen's great impersonators. In 2012 the British actor, 55, took on the task of embodying a man whose flesh has been turned into marble by 150 years of mythologizing, Abraham Lincoln.

Tall, hawk-nosed and commanding, Day-Lewis offered the perfect canvas for director Steven Spielberg's makeup artists, and he emerged as the spit and image of the 16th President. "Day-Lewis' physical resemblance to Lincoln is uncanny," declared TIME's Lily Rothman. As for *Lincoln,* Spielberg's adaptation of historian Doris Kearns Goodwin's popular 2005 study *Team of Rivals,* readers will have to judge for themselves: the film opened after this book went to press.

### PHILIP SEYMOUR HOFFMAN AS LANCASTER DODD

The widely esteemed Hoffman, 45, assumed the role of shaman-showman Dodd, modeled loosely on Scientology founder L. Ron Hubbard, in director Paul Thomas Anderson's *The Master.* Result: he shared the Best Actor nod at the Venice Film Festival with Joaquin Phoenix, who played his apprentice. TIME's Corliss observed that "in Hoffman's lovely impersonation, [Dodd] is less Old Nick than Saint Nick," but found the film a tad too long. "For many viewers, there will be boredom."

### EMMA WATSON AS SAM

She grew up before our eyes playing wizard-in-training Hermione Granger for 10 years in the *Harry Potter* series, but it's still surprising to recall that British ingenue Watson only turned 22 in 2012. For her first role since bidding farewell to Hogwarts, Watson thought small, choosing a low-key, low-budget film based on a popular young-adult novel, *The Perks of Being a Wallflower,* in which she played Sam, an American high school girl. TIME's Corliss concluded, "Watson makes a smooth matriculation from the England-made *Harry Potter* epics to this movie's thrifty, six-week Pittsburgh shoot."

CLOCKWISE FROM TOP: DAVID JAMES—SMPSP/DREAMWORKS; JOHN BRAMLEY—©SUMMIT ENTERTAINMENT/ EVERETT COLLECTION; PHIL BRAY—©THE WEINSTEIN COMPANY/EVERETT COLLECTION

# Joss Whedon

## Hollywood's subversive director takes the reins of a cartoon empire

**A** POPULAR T-SHIRT AT COMICS AND SCIENCE-fiction conventions reads, in the famous *Star Wars* font, JOSS WHEDON IS MY MASTER NOW. The implication is along the order of "George Lucas used to be the gold standard for pure authentic nerd awesomeness, but he betrayed us by making that crappy prequel trilogy. The torch has been passed. Now I'm putting my faith in Joss Whedon."

Whedon, 47, is best known as the creator of the cult fantasy-horror series *Buffy the Vampire Slayer,* as well as TV's beloved but short-lived *Firefly* and *Dollhouse.* More than anybody else, Whedon is the voice of the fan in Hollywood. He's the outsider who lives and works on the inside, in the heart of the heartless studio system. "I will never put something out that I don't believe in," he says. "Everything I've ever worked on, I loved on some level. And yes, I'm including *Waterworld.*" Yet in 2012 the rebel took on the super-hero colossus film *The Avengers,* which he wrote and directed for the big screen—and, earning more than $1.4 billion, it became the year's No. 1 blockbuster.

As a cult figure, Whedon was an odd choice to direct *The Avengers;* he's a known subversive whose modus operandi is to undermine the status quo and aggres-sively deconstruct whatever genre he's working in. In choosing him to direct a $200 million movie, Marvel Comics handed over its icons to an iconoclast.

Whedon may be an iconoclast, but he has deep roots in Hollywood. In fact, he may be the only living third-generation screenwriter: his father wrote for *Dick Cavett* and *The Golden Girls,* and his grandfather was a writer for Andy Griffith and Dick Van Dyke. He began his career in 1989, writing for mainstream TV—first for *Roseanne,* then *Parenthood.* He went on to become something of a pop-culture Zelig, contrib-uting to the scripts of *Toy Story, Waterworld, Speed, Twister* and more. In the past five years he has directed episodes of *The Office* and *Glee.* In April 2012 he was in the unusual position of having two movies premier-ing in Los Angeles on consecutive days: *Cabin in the Woods,* an inside-out, meta-horror flick he co-wrote and produced, followed by *The Avengers.* Incredibly, Whedon already had yet another film in postproduc-tion as of early 2012, a larky low-budget take on *Much Ado About Nothing* that he shot in a month with a cast of his favorite actors. Chances are it will be the first film about nothing to create some ado. ■

—*By Lev Grossman*

MATT CARR—GETTY IMAGES

# E.L. James

## Purple prose, gobs of greenbacks and *Fifty Shades of Grey*

**S**EX AFTER MARRIAGE, THE OLD SAYING goes, has three phases: kitchen, bedroom and hallway. Kitchen sex is the spontaneous type spouses have when they first get together. Bedroom sex is the more routine lovemaking that sets in after a few years. And hallway sex is when husband and wife pass each other in the hallway and say, "Screw you."

In 2012, however, millions of readers discovered a fourth kind: the sex that hallway-phase couples start having after the wife reads novels by E.L. James, a virtual unknown—even in the wildly lucrative but disdained romance genre. Until recently James was posting her stories online for free, and she readily acknowledges that they are heavily based on another person's work. Yet her trilogy *Fifty Shades of Grey, Fifty Shades Darker* and *Fifty Shades Freed,* um, dominated both the hardbound and e-book best-seller lists and was auctioned to Hollywood in a seven-figure deal. Why the flush of interest? Reducing the women of America to quivering masses of desire, the books sparked a new genre of fiction: "mommy porn."

In her other life, James is Erika Leonard, 49, a Nutella-loving wife and mother of teen boys, who, prefame, worked in the nonglamorous end of TV production, organizing contracts and clearances. To escape, the Briton used to read a lot of romance novels—she still has about 700 of them in her attic—and began writing fan fiction on the Internet. Indeed, the *Fifty Shades* series began as a piece of fan fiction based on the *Twilight* series by Stephenie Meyer. While her books are racy, Leonard is rather shy and prudish. She giggled, horrified, when asked to read aloud from one of the steamier passages she has written.

The novels follow the romantic education of Anastasia Steele, a klutzy, frizzy-haired university student and hardware-store worker from Portland, Ore., and Christian Grey, a formidably wealthy Seattle entrepreneur who falls for her when she interviews him for her school paper. What keeps these two from instantly getting together? Paperwork. Grey dearly wishes that Ms. Steele, as he often calls her, would sign a nondisclosure agreement as well as a contract in which she agrees to let him control everything she eats and wears and to let him "flog, spank, whip or corporally punish" her as he sees fit. And she can't ever touch him.

Ms. Steele is a 21-year-old modern student with no computer, no smartphone and no e-mail. She's not only virginal; she's Cro-Magnon. But thanks to her story, 2012 was publishing's Year of James: the year when Anastasia Steele discovered her libidinous inner goddess and mainstream America discovered S&M. As for James, in dealing with the U.S. publishing-and-media colossus, she was just like her heroine, the e-mail-less virgin, trying to decide whether to hitch her wagon to this new suitor with his peculiar appetites.

Spoiler alert: She's all in. ∎

*—By Belinda Luscombe*

ROGER CREMERS—HOLLANDSE HOOGTE/REDUX

# Hot Tickets. Broadway musicals go folksy and pop music gets giddy

## ONCE

Adapted from a low-budget 2006 Irish film that focused on scruffy, folk-singing street buskers, *Once* seemed unlikely to become a Broadway smash. But critics and audiences loved the heartfelt stage adaptation, which garnered eight Tony Awards in 2012, including Best Musical, Best Actor and Best Book. Below, sparks fly between Steve Kazee and Cristin Milioti.

## NEWSIES

Digging deep into the company's vast studio vault, the imagineers at the Walt Disney Co. rebooted a poorly received 1992 film about New York City newsboys on strike in 1899 into a popular hit. TIME critic Richard Zoglin dissented, declaring the musical "as disposable as yesterday's newspaper ... [and] drawn with Crayola—the old boxes with just eight colors."

## PORGY AND BESS

This new production of the legendary 1935 "folk opera" struck sparks of controversy even before it opened. Approved by the estates of composer George Gershwin and his lyricist brother Ira, the musical was billed as *The Gershwins' Porgy and Bess* and was described as an attempt to create a stripped-down, more modern version of an unwieldy classic. Many critics frowned, but audiences approved—and no one disputed that Broadway veteran Audra McDonald was one of history's great Besses.

## THE ICEMAN COMETH

Chicago's Goodman Theatre, one of the nation's great playhouses, mounted a powerful staging of Eugene O'Neill's epic drama about self-deluded barflies, directed by Robert Falls. The strong cast included Brian Dennehy, left, as Larry Slade and Nathan Lane as the play's mainspring, Theodore ("Hickey") Hickman.

CLOCKWISE FROM TOP LEFT: T. CHARLES ERICKSON/DISNEY THEATRICAL./AP; JOAN MARCUS/BONEAU/BRYAN-BROWN/ AP IMAGES; AP PHOTO/COURTESY OF THE GOODMAN THEATRE, LIZ LAUREN; ANDREW H. WALKER/WIREIMAGE

## CARLY RAE JEPSEN

Maybe it was a reaction to the torchy ballads of Adele that ruled pop in 2011. Whatever the reason, 2012 turned out to be long on fluff in popular music. One of the year's inescapable hits was *Canadian Idol* veteran Carly Rae Jepsen's cutesy ode to her cell phone, *Call Me Maybe*. Boosted by the endorsement of fellow Canadian superstar Justin Bieber, Jepsen, 26, found her video for the song parodied by an unlikely and wide-ranging roster of imitators, including members of the U.S. Olympic swimming and diving teams. Rolling in the shallows, anyone?

## FRANK OCEAN

For hip-hop star Frank Ocean, 2012 was a coming-out party in more ways than one. With the release of his CD *Channel Orange* in July, the man who had sung back-up for Beyoncé, Jay-Z and Kanye West emerged as a gifted writer and singer in his own right, creating rich, hook-filled tracks with heart-wrenching lyrics.

Just before the album's release, Ocean, 24, revealed that his first love was a man— a courageous revelation in a genre that is not known for being inclusive of homosexuality.

## PSY

Some years are recalled for nutty dance crazes: Remember doing the *Macarena* in 1996? In 2012, Korean rapper Park Jae-sang, a.k.a. Psy, put the giddy in giddy-up with the video for his smash hit *Gangnam Style,* featuring the 34-year-old's goofy "horse dance." Above, Psy hoofs it for NBC's *Today* show at Rockefeller Center in New York City. His emergence, certified 2012-style by more than 300 million views of the video on YouTube, was a breakout moment for South Korean pop culture, or K-pop.

CLOCKWISE FROM TOP: JEFF FUSCO—GETTY IMAGES; KEVORK DJANSEZIAN—GETTY IMAGES; JASON DECROW—INVISION/AP; BARRY BRECHEISEN—WIREIMAGE

## ADELE

The soulful British singer Adele (Adkins), who turned 24 in 2012, spent the year reaping the rewards of her unstoppable 2011 release *21,* powered by the churning single *Rolling in the Deep*. In an era when CD sales are dwindling owing to online purchases, the *21* CD sold more than 20 million copies. At the 2012 Grammy Awards, Adele cradled six golden gramophones, practicing a pose she will need in 2013; she announced she was pregnant in June 2012.

# In Brief

## Hello, Columbus

**ART** Even in a city known for its ultracool apartments, this living room seemed to have it all: sixth-floor views of Central Park, hip contemporary design—and a 13-ft. (4 m) -tall sculpture of Christopher Columbus standing on the coffee table. Then again, the space wasn't really an apartment: it was an art installation, "Discovering Columbus," designed by Japanese artist Tatzu Nishi.

The work involved building a full living room around a 19th century statue of the explorer, which is perched atop a 60-ft. (18 m) granite column in Manhattan's bustling Columbus Circle, at the southwest corner of Central Park. The installation is shown under construction below. More than 100,000 people were expected to discover Columbus—and the fictional apartment of his wealthy owner—during the exhibit's two-month run.

**NUMBERS**

# 4,000

*Number of women Mick Jagger has bedded thus far, according to a 2012 biography by Chris Andersen. Among the Rolling Stone's most notable (alleged) conquests: Farrah Fawcett, Angelina Jolie and Uma Thurman*

# $7

*Price a woman paid at a West Virginia yard sale for a box of trinkets. Surprise! In the box was a painting by Renoir that had been stolen from the Baltimore Museum of Art in 1951*

## Heroine of a Thousand Faces

**PHOTOGRAPHY** Cindy Sherman takes pictures only of herself, but she always insists she doesn't make self-portraits. It would be truer to say that for the past 35 years, she's been producing a portrait of her times as they flow through the finely tuned instrument of her baroque psyche. Again and again in her spine-tingling retrospective, which opened at the Museum of Modern Art in New York City, and will travel to San Francisco, Minneapolis and Dallas, you also discover she's made a portrait of you.

Growing up in a New York suburb, Sherman loved to play dress-up. In 1977, when she was 23 and just out of Buffalo State College, she started playing it with a vengeance. For three years, she photographed herself in costumes, wigs and settings that drew from the deep pool of movie images we're all immersed in from childhood. In what eventually grew to a series of 70 "Untitled Film Stills," she took on the roles of career girl, housewife, siren and others.

By 1995, when MOMA reportedly paid what was then the newsmaking sum of $1 million for a full set of the stills, Sherman, above, was established as one of the pivotal artists of her generation. That's also Sherman below, in *Untitled #465,* in character as one of a series of brittle, aging beauties with money that the artist began embodying in 2008.

CLOCKWISE FROM TOP LEFT: ANN HERMES—THE CHRISTIAN SCIENCE MONITOR/GETTYIMAGES; CHARLES ESHELMAN—FILMMAGIC/GETTY IMAGES; COURTESY THE ARTIST AND METRO PICTURES, NEW YORK, ©2012; MARCUS YAM—THE NEW YORK TIMES/REDUX

CLOCKWISE FROM TOP: FLOTO+WARNER; NO CREDIT; HOLLY ANDRES—TIME; KENT SMITH—SHOWTIME

## Free at Last, a Great Collection Has a New Home

**ART** *For much of his life, the spectacularly cranky Albert C. Barnes, a wealthy chemist, was at war with the social élites of Philadelphia. In the 1920s, many of them had no taste for the Cézannes, Matisses, van Goghs and Picassos at his private museum, a limestone villa located in the suburb of Merion, Pa. But as tastes evolved after Barnes' death in 1951, Philadelphians began to dream of bringing his magnificent collection of masterpieces into town. After a long-running drama, the funds were raised to do so, and in 2012 the new Barnes Foundation museum opened. Its rooms, by court order, carefully duplicate the interior of Barnes' original building. But thanks to the design by New York City–based architects Tod Williams and Billie Tsien, the new/old museum displays its treasures in spectacular, yet subtle, fashion.*

## From a Vast Wasteland to a Potent *Homeland*

**TELEVISION** Not so long ago, it was still fashionable to complain about the dearth of good programs on TV. But in the years since HBO's breakthrough series *The Sopranos* proved the power and appeal of long-form narrative drama filmed for the small screen, television—and cable television in particular—has become a rich source of quality entertainment for grownups. The nominees for Outstanding Drama Series at the 2012 Primetime Emmy Awards constituted a golden age of TV brilliance: *Boardwalk Empire* (HBO), *Homeland* (Showtime), *Breaking Bad* (AMC), *Downton Abbey* (PBS), *Game of Thrones* (HBO) and *Mad Men* (AMC).

And the Emmy went to: *Homeland,* a bracing, absorbing thriller about contemporary domestic terrorism starring Claire Danes, above, and Damian Lewis. Comedy was also stirring on the tube. Louis C.K.'s *Louie* (FX) and HBO's compelling comedy/drama *Girls,* starring its creator, 26-year-old Lena Dunham, demonstrated that quirky, original voices could move comedy past that wheezy old format, the sitcom.

## Hiker, Heal Thyself

**BOOKS** For many book lovers, 2012 was the Year of Strayed, as onetime novelist Cheryl Strayed, 43, won hearts and minds with a one-two punch of compelling nonfiction. Her memoir *Wild,* published in March, tells the story of her solo trek along the Pacific Crest Trail when she was 26, a journey she undertook to help her recover from two overwhelming griefs: the loss of her mother four years earlier to cancer and the breakup of her marriage. Well received when published, it hit No. 1 on the best-seller lists in the summer, thanks to Oprah Winfrey, who made it the first pick of her latest book club.

In July Strayed released *Tiny Beautiful Things,* a collection of new-wave takes on an old format, the advice column. An anecdotal memoir in disguise, its entries first appeared in the online literary journal the *Rumpus.*

# Milestones

FROM LEFT, NASA/ROGER RESSMEYER-CORBIS; DEBORAH FEINGOLD—
CORBIS OUTLINE; DAVID CORIO—REDFERNS/GETTY IMAGES

"All I'm armed with is research." —Mike Wallace

A TRIO OF LEGENDS

*Left: Apollo 11 astronauts Buzz Aldrin, on left, and Neil Armstrong place the American flag on the moon on July 20, 1969.*
*Middle: CBS journalist Mike Wallace of* 60 Minutes *is shown in his New York City office in 1984.*
*Right: Whitney Houston sings at London's Wembley Arena in 1988.*

# Neil Armstrong

A quiet but gutsy hero, the combat veteran and test pilot
left his mark on the moon—and on his home planet

**N**EIL ARMSTRONG WAS A MAN OF ALMOST preternatural imperturbability. That, of course, is true of all of astronauts—especially those from the 1960s. He, like so many others, started out as a military pilot. His service included 78 combat missions over Korea, during one of which his plane was crippled by antiaircraft fire. He managed to stay airborne long enough to limp back into American-held territory before he bailed out. He retired from the Navy after the war and became a test pilot for the National Advisory Committee for Aeronautics (NASA's predecessor) and flew 900 different types of aircraft—all of them fit only for test pilots because no one could predict whether the things would perform as designed or would shake themselves into rivets once they reached flight speed.

It wasn't until 1962 that Armstrong joined NASA—in the second crop of astronauts chosen after the glorious Original Seven. On at least three occasions that followed, the machines he flew tried to kill him. On March 16, 1966, Armstrong and crewmate David Scott rode Gemini 8 to orbit, launching what was intended to be a five-day mission; instead, it lasted little more than 10 hours. After their craft docked with an unmanned one for practice, the paired ships began spinning out of control, barrel-rolling at one revolution per second. Armstrong shut down his module's main thrusters, fired up the backup system and brought his bucking spacecraft to heel.

Two years later, Armstrong was flying a far more ignoble machine: the ugly, insectile Lunar Landing Training Vehicle (LLTV). The 22-ft. (6.7 m), 2,500-lb. (1,100 kg), four-legged contraption was not built to climb much more than 1,000 ft. (300 m) off the ground. On May 6, 1968, Armstrong had the thing just a few hundred feet in the air at Ellington Air Force Base in Texas when it stopped responding to his commands, violently swinging first one way, then the other. When the LLTV went into a straight, shallow dive, it was clear the game was over. Armstrong ejected, the LLTV

crashed, and he descended gently to the ground, passing directly through the oily cloud of black smoke the wrecked machine was giving off. An hour later, astronaut Al Bean heard the news and dashed over to Armstrong's Ellington office, where he found the future first man on the moon sitting at his desk, filing paperwork.

It was the lunar module *Eagle* that nearly took out Armstrong the final time, when he and Buzz Aldrin were making their final approach to their Tranquility Base landing site on July 20, 1969. Suddenly the warning-panel flashed: the lander's computer system was overloaded and could process no more. At the same time, the module, or LEM, was exceedingly, dangerously low on fuel. Below the craft, an unexpected boulder field loomed ever closer. Armstrong took the stick from the harried computer, tilted the half-upright LEM into a head-forward lean and flew across the boulders to a safe touchdown. There were, NASA engineers later calculated, about 30 seconds of fuel left in the tank.

## After flying 78 combat missions in Korea, Armstrong eluded death twice more on Earth— and once more on the moon

Armstrong, Aldrin and Michael Collins came home heroes—Armstrong the greatest among them. After retiring from NASA in 1971, he began teaching at the University of Cincinnati, delivered speeches when he absolutely had to and served, when called—notably on the investigation panels after the near disaster of Apollo 13 and the true disaster of the shuttle *Challenger*. He was only 38 when he walked on the moon, but he surely knew that if he lived to be 100, his life would forever be defined by the 151 minutes he spent on its surface. There was a lot to mourn when Armstrong died on Aug. 25 at 82—most of all the loss of a man who had carried himself with such silent grace for so many years. ■

—*By Jeffrey Kluger*

**Outward bound** *Armstrong confers with spacesuit technicians a few days before the Apollo 11 mission blasted off for the moon on July 16, 1969*

CENTRAL PRESS/GETTY IMAGES

**Pioneer** *Ride, the first U.S. woman in space, checks out the flight deck of the space shuttle* Challenger *before her historic 1983 flight*

## Sally Ride
Blasting through a glass ceiling, she broke new ground for women

SALLY RIDE WAS NOT OLD ENOUGH TO HAVE applied for a spot at NASA in the days when women in the space community were either wives, daughters, groupies or spacesuit seamstresses. But she surely was old enough to understand the sting those woman felt; old enough to know that while the NASA of the 1950s made a pro forma gesture of considering female applicants for the astronaut corps, those same women were the object of eye-rolls at best, jokes or disdain at worst. Their applications were accepted simply as an act of bureaucratic box-checking.

By the mid-1970s that had changed just enough that Ride could apply to the shuttle program—one of 8,000 astronaut candidates given consideration. By 1978, she was named part of an incoming astronaut class that included five other women and 29 men. They were referred to around NASA as "the 35 new guys," and if the six who didn't quite fit that description minded, they

said nothing. When she climbed into *Challenger* on June 18, 1983, and the hatch was closed and sealed behind her, a far bigger cultural door opened—and every American woman who has since flown a military plane or a commercial jet or a spacecraft followed her through it.

Ride flew into space a second time, in 1984, also aboard *Challenger*. It was thus fitting that she was named to the panel that investigated the explosion of the ship during its ascent in 1986. The Stanford grad with a Ph.D. in physics left NASA in 1987 to teach at Stanford and later at the University of California, San Diego. In 2001, she founded Sally Ride Science, aiming to encourage children, especially girls, to pursue science careers. She died at 61 in July 2012, after a long battle with pancreatic cancer that she did not divulge to the public. Always a private person, she also chose to keep her relationship with her partner of 27 years, Tam O'Shaughnessy, a secret until her death. ∎

HARRY BENSON—CONTOUR/GETTY IMAGES

# Mike Wallace

## A passionate seeker of the truth, he brought high drama to television news

**M**IKE WALLACE AND *60 MINUTES* WERE THE perfect marriage of man and medium. The great news producer Don Hewitt brilliantly paired the combative Wallace with the reassuring Harry Reasoner to launch his television newsmagazine in 1968. Mike, who was 93 when he died in April 2012, helped invent a distinctive style of fearless reporting that was perfectly suited to this new genre.

Wallace's so-called ambush interviews with assorted villains lingered in the popular imagination years after he stopped doing them. His encounters with world leaders, celebrities and scoundrels—or combinations of the three—built the program's reputation for unflinching pursuit of the truth on the viewers' behalf. Think about it: if a correspondent is willing to ask the Ayatullah Khomeini whether he is a lunatic, as Mike famously did, he'll ask anyone anything. And even as *60 Minutes*

became an all-star team of television news greats— Ed Bradley, Morley Safer, Dan Rather, Lesley Stahl, Diane Sawyer, Andy Rooney—Mike's colleagues always acknowledged him as its on-air personification.

Mike was the same man off camera as on: challenging, mischievous, fearsome yet vulnerable. He struggled with personal tragedy, including the loss of a son, and he wasn't afraid to show vulnerability, eventually revealing years of struggle with depression. Like the late Andy Rooney, he was the real human being he appeared to be. While so much television news has become the blond leading the bland, Mike was colorful and unapologetically a showman—but always in the name of the story. He wielded righteous indignation years before doing so became cool on cable, and he served no ideology other than practicing great television journalism. ■

*—By Andrew Heyward, CBS News president, 1996-2005*

CBS/LANDOV

**Two for the road** *Wallace was at home with both the famous and infamous; he hitched a ride with tenor Luciano Pavarotti in 1993*

**Visionary** *The writer in 1982. His vision was so poor that his Coke-bottle spectacles became his signature—and he never learned to drive*

# Ray Bradbury

"I don't try to describe the future," the author declared, "I try to prevent it"

MORE THAN FANTASY OR EVEN SCIENCE fiction, horror was Ray Bradbury's primary mode, and like so many great horror writers, he was himself utterly without fear, of anything. He wasn't afraid of looking uncool; he wasn't scared to openly love innocence, or to be optimistic, or to write sentimentally when he felt that way. He wrote beautifully enough for adults and clearly enough for kids. He didn't give a damn if the literary lions accepted him—"If I'd found out that Norman Mailer liked me," he once said, "I'd have killed myself." He wrote in any and every genre, including poetry. His advice to writers—and it's among the best ever given—is as follows: "You've got to jump off cliffs all the time and build your wings on the way down."

Bradbury was born in 1920 in Waukegan, Ill. It was the early days of science fiction and fantasy, so he grew up reading Poe and L. Frank Baum and Edgar Rice Burroughs. The family moved to Los Angeles in 1934, but that idyllic small Midwestern city always remained Bradbury's home planet. You feel the gravitational pull of it in everything he wrote—an American Eden, though not without its snakes.

Bradbury was an early crossover figure, a science-fiction/fantasy/horror writer whose stylistic abilities were so obvious, and whose thematic range was so deep and powerful, that he became unclassifiable. He was a creature of the pulps who was taught in universities and published in *Esquire* and who wrote in any format that caught his eye. He was the shape of things to come—Kurt Vonnegut, Philip K. Dick, Michael Chabon and Neil Gaiman would all follow in the path he cleared. A cliff-jumper all his life, Bradbury never hit the ground; he died peacefully, at 91, in Los Angeles in June 2012. ∎

—*By Lev Grossman*

LENOX MCLENDON—AP

# Maurice Sendak

## A Magellan of inner space, he charted the geography of children's minds

**A**N ETERNAL TWILIGHT REIGNS OVER MAU-rice Sendak's pages: dark cross-hatching, thick outlines, ominous skies. All his characters, human and beast alike, are lumpy and big-headed and seem to be part potato. But they're capable of great joy in spite of it all. They kick up their heavy limbs and grin toothy grins as if to say, Yes, the world is dark. We're going to have a damn good time of it anyway. Let the wild rumpus start!

Born in Brooklyn in 1928 to Jewish immigrants from Poland, Sendak grew up haunted by the Holocaust, which claimed lives in his extended Polish family. He was inspired to become an artist after seeing Walt Disney's *Fantasia,* and he first won attention as an illustrator of children's books written by other authors—including Else Holmelund Minarik's *Little Bear* series—before he began writing his own tales. Published in 1963, his classic, *Where the Wild Things Are,* turned the old

story about monsters in the closet on its head by making a little boy the biggest monster in the jungle. It was Sendak's way of saying that children already know where the wild things are, because they're the wildest things of all.

In 1972, Sendak told renowned children's librarian Virginia Haviland that he didn't understand why pretend play is considered child's play. "I believe there is no part of our lives, our adult as well as child life, when we're not fantasizing, but we prefer to relegate fantasy to children, as though it were some tomfoolery only fit for the immature minds of the young."

Sendak died at 83 in May 2012. Over the years, his art made its way into every medium—movies, operas, ballet—but he was best known for his picture books, which never participate in the adult conspiracy that forces kids to pretend they don't already know how hard life is. "I refuse to lie to children," Sendak said in a 2011 interview. "I refuse to cater to the bull---- of 'innocence.' " ■

**Wild things** *Sendak poses with a friend of his creation in 1985; he designed sets for a wide range of opera, ballet and theater companies*

## Whitney Houston

# Her voice was uplifting, but personal demons brought her down

**S**HE WAS BORN TO SING. HER MOTHER WAS Cissy Houston, a soul and gospel performer who sang backup for Elvis Presley, Mahalia Jackson and Aretha Franklin. Her cousin was Dionne Warwick, one of the indelible voices of American pop. Whitney Elizabeth Houston was singing in the choir in her hometown of Newark, N.J., at age 11. Her beauty led to an early modeling career, but her vocal talents soon led to a contract with Arista Records producer Clive Davis, who would do more than anyone to shape her public image.

That image was of the gorgeous all-American girl who could belt ballads and dance tunes with equal ease. In the beginning, she was perfectly cast: glamorous and distant, with a voice that was warm, even if the celebrity was unapproachable. She made you move; she made you want; she gave immediacy and voice to your instincts and emotions. She was a goddess.

Beginning in 1985, that goddess would produce pop hit after pop hit: *Saving All My Love for You, How Will I Know, I Wanna Dance with Somebody (Who Loves Me)*. Her cover of Dolly Parton's *I Will Always Love You* overshadowed the original. Her first major foray into the movie industry in *The Bodyguard* (1992) was a smash hit. The range and power of her natural gifts produced at the 1991 Super Bowl—with the U.S. 10 days into the first Gulf War—one of the most astonishing renditions of *The Star-Spangled Banner* ever heard. The U.S. Air Force planes flying overhead became a mere afterthought to her renewal of the vigor of words written in 1814. She was the voice of America.

Her sad decline began after her marriage to one of the bad boys of the industry, Bobby Brown. That union, which lasted from 1992 to 2007, would be rocked by rumors of infidelity and drug use. In her last few years, Houston looked haggard and worn; her face both puffy and emaciated. More tragically, her voice was shattered, no longer able to soar. On Feb. 11, 2012, at age 48, she was found dead in the bathtub of a Los Angeles hotel room just one day before the Grammy Awards ceremony. A coroner's report found that heart disease and cocaine use contributed to her death. ■

—*By Howard Chua-Eoan*

**Houston in 1988**

**What's new, pussycat?** *Brown savors the good life in 1965, when she first took the reins at* Cosmopolitan

# Helen Gurley Brown

## Breathing life into the Cosmo Girl, she helped lead a revolution

LEFT: GRAHAM WILTSHIRE—CAMERA PRESS/REDUX; RIGHT: CORBIS/BETTMANN

**H**ER UNIVERSAL TERM OF ENDEARMENT WAS "pussycat"—warm, fuzzy yet still feline, with all that's feral in the pet implicit. Helen Gurley Brown coined another word, "mouseburger," which applied to a timid woman that a pussycat can presumably feed on and spit out, the opposite of the Cosmo Girl idealized by the magazine she edited for more than three decades. Mouseburger was originally her description of herself—a woman born neither beautiful nor powerful. But as one of publishing's most colorful and controversial pioneers, Brown made herself influential and attractive, a big cat to be reckoned with in the concrete jungle.

Brown, who died at 90 in August 2012, recognized the consumer marketability of the female libidinal instinct in its quest for romantic happiness. She turned *Cosmopolitan* into a manifesto of that combination—a feat that both pleased and appalled feminists who saw liberation in weightier terms. To them, the *Cosmopolitan* ethos is a fatally limited one. But it is persistent.

Born Helen Gurley on Feb. 18, 1922, in Green Forest,

Ark., she began her career as a secretary and advertising copywriter. She became a household name and best-selling author in 1962 with the publication of her first book, *Sex and the Single Girl*. Offering witty tips on everything from decorating to dieting, and addressing sex frankly, the book became an instant blockbuster that sold 2 million copies in three weeks. Brown arrived at a struggling *Cosmopolitan* magazine in 1965 without a college degree or previous editing experience. The magazine's first female editor in chief tripled its circulation, coining the "fun, fearless, female" moniker and unapologetically featuring sex, skin and splash on its pages.

In her own love life, Brown didn't need any manuals—she wed film producer David Brown in 1959, and the two remained married until his death in 2010. Her boldness and brashness emboldened generations of women, up to a point: feminist author Gloria Steinem told the New York *Times* that "*Cosmo* became the unliberated woman's survival kit, with advice on how to please a man, lover or boss under any circumstances." ∎

# Joe Paterno

## A coach revered for his high ideals suffered a self-inflicted fall from grace

WE ALL THOUGHT HIS CAREER WOULD END with a coronation. Joe Paterno, who led Penn State University's football team to two national championships and five undefeated seasons in his almost 46 years as head coach, whose players bucked the college-jock stereotype and consistently earned diplomas, was supposed to leave the sidelines on his terms and be properly feted as one of the best the game has ever seen. But Paterno never got his grand send-off. Instead, just days after winning his 409th game, the most of any head coach in major college-football history, his career ended under a dark, unfathomable cloud. A little more than two months after that, his life ended as well.

Paterno, who died of complications from lung cancer on Jan. 22, 2012, at 85, was fired in November 2011, primarily for failing in 2001 to report to police the allegations of child sexual abuse against his former longtime defensive coach Jerry Sandusky. Paterno fulfilled his legal obligation by reporting the accusations to his immediate superiors, but Penn State's board of trustees, and much of the public, felt that a coach so celebrated for doing the right thing suffered a grave lapse in moral judgment. "I wish I had done more," Paterno admitted after his dismissal, which caused a minor riot on campus.

In the wake of the scandal, Paterno was removed from consideration for the Presidential Medal of Freedom. His name was scrubbed off the trophy given every year to the football champion of the Big Ten Conference, and the celebrated life-size statue of him running onto the field was removed from outside Beaver Stadium.

For Paterno, the scandal was a crushing final chapter to a celebrated life. He was born in Brooklyn, studied Latin at Brooklyn Prep, a now defunct Jesuit school, and majored in English literature at Brown, where he played quarterback and cornerback. He said Virgil's *Aeneid,* the epic poem about a courageous Trojan hero, "probably had as much influence on me as anything in my life." Paterno loved football, and Penn State, so much that he suspected he would literally die without the Nittany Lions in his veins. The premonition proved eerily true. But no one saw him dying as a tragic figure. ■

—*By Sean Gregory*

**A legend no more** *Paterno—a familiar figure in rolled-up khakis and thick eyeglasses—departed in disgrace from the game he loved*

PAT LITTLE—AP

**Advocate for peace** *Senator McGovern campaigns in California in June 1972 for the Democratic presidential nomination*

# George McGovern
## A World War II veteran, he ran for the presidency on an anti-war platform

IN THE HISTORY OF LOST CAUSES, THE FIGURE of George McGovern casts a poignant shadow. The South Dakota Senator's run for the White House in 1972 ended in one of the biggest electoral defeats in American presidential history. The Democrat's unalloyed opposition to the Vietnam War, his unapologetic espousal of the concept of income redistribution, his belief that government was a solution to America's problems, his unrepentant liberalism—all formed part of what was even then a quixotic campaign.

Opposition to America's military support of South Vietnam was at the heart of McGovern's campaign. And he brought to his stance a certainty born of experience. The South Dakota native volunteered to fight for his country in World War II and, as a pilot, flew bombing missions over Nazi-occupied Europe. He returned to serve two terms in the House (1957-61) before joining the Senate in 1963. His views on the Vietnam War crystallized during his first term as Senator, although he initially publicly supported the actions of President Lyndon Johnson in Vietnam, including voting in favor of the Gulf of Tonkin Resolution in 1964, authorizing the escalation of the war. He would later regret the vote.

By 1969 McGovern was demanding the withdrawal of U.S. troops from the Southeast Asian country. His positions, including criticism of South Vietnamese corruption, were perceived as radical in a country that still mostly believed it was a patriotic duty to stand by a U.S. government at war. In the 1972 campaign, his judgment was called into question when his first choice as Veep—Thomas Eagleton—was forced to withdraw after confessing to having had electroshock therapy for depression. Campaign funds dried up as McGovern's poll numbers showed no sign of lifting. Finally, the enthusiastic youth vote he counted on did not materialize at the polls.

George McGovern died at 90 in October. While his vision of America may have gone down to spectacular defeat in 1972, he remains a quintessentially American figure—intransigently idealistic, fearless in his conviction, tireless in his pursuit of a better vision of the U.S. His admonitions still resonate in the country's conscience with all the wisdom of a veteran of lost causes. "The highest patriotism is not a blind acceptance of official policy," he once declared, "but a love of one's country deep enough to call her to a higher standard." ∎
—*By Howard Chua-Eoan*

BETTMANN/CORBIS

Ephron in 2010

## Nora Ephron
### Jane Austen of a wired world

CHILD OF A HUSBAND-WIFE TEAM OF Hollywood screenwriters, Nora Ephron took up the family trade and enjoyed a brilliant career as novelist, screenwriter, essayist, film director, memoirist and public figure before her death at 71 in June 2012. As a young reporter for the New York *Post* amid the swirl of the 1960s, she acquired a journalist's eye for detail and a wry but wise voice. Actor Tom Hanks, who starred in *Sleepless in Seattle* and *You've Got Mail!*, classic romantic comedies written and directed by Ephron, recalled in an appreciation in TIME: "It was her journalist's curiosity that made Nora the directing talent she was. Her writing was always voice and detail. I once sent her a piece I was trying to write, and her response was three words: 'Voice! Voice! Voice!'"

Like Gore Vidal, Ephron gracefully mastered every medium she took up. She was nominated three times for the Academy Award in screenwriting. As a director, she enjoyed a string of successes that ran through her warm 2010 comedy, *Julie & Julia.* When her second marriage collapsed due to her husband's infidelity, she turned the tale into *Heartburn,* both a best seller and hit film. Her witty, widely admired essay collections chronicled a changing America over four decades, from *Wallflower at the Orgy* in 1970 to *I Remember Nothing* in 2010. In that final book, she revealed her approach to life: "My religion is Get Over It," she declared. ■

## Gore Vidal
### He came, he saw, he skewered

IS THERE A 2012 EQUIVALENT TO THE honorific "man of letters"? The phrase used to refer, with a blithely unconscious sexism, to a writer who took all the world as his page in novels, plays, screenplays and essays, and whose political opinions found listeners beyond the ghetto of the intelligentsia. The years just after World War II produced a host of these public savants: Norman Mailer, Truman Capote, William F. Buckley Jr. and—brawling with and outliving each of them—Gore Vidal, who spent nearly seven decades as a roaring or purring literary lion before dying in July 2012 at 86. His rivals may have written finer, deeper, more penetrating or more influential works, but no other writer could claim Vidal's sheer, breathless breadth: authorship of best-selling historical novels *(Burr, Lincoln),* a scandalous transsexual jape *(Myra Breckinridge),* a classic play on American politics *(The Best Man)* and the most expensive pornographic film ever made *(Caligula).*

Vidal earned his own form of notoriety with 1948's *The City and the Pillar,* one of the first novels on the subject of homosexuality. This coming-of-age story was also a coming-out confessional. Vidal lived for 53 years with advertising executive Howard Austen, though, ever a maverick, he averred that he and Austen were not sexual partners. Asked a few years ago about gay marriage, Vidal replied, "Since heterosexual marriage is such a disaster, why on earth would anybody want to imitate it?" ■

—*By Richard Corliss*

Vidal in 1968

FROM LEFT: LUCAS JACKSON—REUTERS; BETTMANN/CORBIS

**Fuentes in 1973**

FROM LEFT: SOPHIE BASSOULS—SYGMA/CORBIS; EVERETT COLLECTION

## Carlos Fuentes
### Capturing a Mexico torn between lofty visions and squalid realities

CARLOS FUENTES' BEST-KNOWN NOVEL may be *The Old Gringo* (1985), set during the Mexican Revolution. But his finest fiction dwelled in the aftermath of that upheaval, wryly but passionately decrying modern Mexico's betrayals of the revolution's egalitarian values. Few characters embody that venality more than Artemio Cruz, the soldier-politico-tycoon who haunts *The Death of Artemio Cruz* (1962), the finest of Fuentes' 24 novels and a masterly portrait of the one-party dictatorship that ruled Mexico for most of the 20th century.

Fuentes, who died at 83 in May 2012, co-founded Latin America's literary boom, a movement that included his Nobel-laureate buddies Gabriel García Márquez and Mario Vargas Llosa, who summoned modernist, magical-realist styles to tell their region's epic. "In the 1960s, why not?" Fuentes once told me. "We were young, bold, infinitely ambitious." And leftist, fired in those days by a Castroesque zeal that made getting U.S. visas a pain. As the cold war gave way to NAFTA, Fuentes soured on "yesterday's communism without freedom" while keeping a keen eye on "today's capitalism without justice." He died knowing that Mexico had finally democratized and reached out to the world. Thanks to Fuentes, the world had already been introduced to the rich if enigmatic soul of Mexico. ∎

*—By Tim Padgett*

## Adrienne Rich
### A poet on society's front lines

ADRIENNE RICH BEGAN HER LONG BEATIfication in American letters at age 22, when her first collection won the 1951 Yale Younger Poets prize. *A Change of World* was a prescient title, for Rich, who died in March 2012 at 82, went on to lead a renaissance in women's writing. "My politics is in my body," she wrote decades later, well aware that she'd won the oppression trifecta— feminist, lesbian, Jewish. But she shouldn't be ghettoized as a political scribe.

I first fell in love with *Diving into the Wreck* (1973) in college for its carnality and canny use of metaphor as much as its ideology. Only three contemporary women poets graced the anthologies I was reading back then, and the other two were suicides.

Throughout the years, Rich remained ambivalent about prizes—accepting the MacArthur, the Bollingen and a National Book Foundation medal but refusing a 1997 National Medal of Arts in protest of certain Clinton Administration policies. Still, while hearing her 2006 NBF acceptance speech, I found myself scribbling one sentence onto scratch paper. It was a brisk, gorgeous blast at popular, decorative verse that insists on self-conscious frivolity. "Poetry is not a healing lotion, an emotional massage, a kind of linguistic aromatherapy." For her it was life's blood—as she was to it, to us. ∎

*—By Mary Karr*

**Rich in 1975**

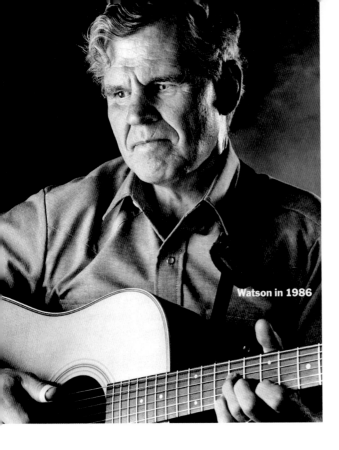

Watson in 1986

## Doc Watson
### He drew music from a deeper well

**B**ORN OF THE MOUNTAINS, ARTHEL ("Doc") Watson grew up in Deep Gap, N.C. Blind since the age of 1, he became interested in music at age 11, when his father brought him a banjo he had made from the skin of a dead cat. The youngster later saved money cutting trees on his family's farm and bought a mail-order guitar; when his rockabilly dance band in the 1950s couldn't afford to hire a fiddle player, Watson learned to flat-pick speedy fiddle solos on his guitar.

His inventiveness became his legacy. Watson's career took off in the early 1960s, when folk music saw a revival. He inspired generations of bluegrass and country artists with his spitfire handling of complex melodies normally reserved for fiddles and banjos, and countless amateur players honed their skills trying to emulate his buoyant sound.

Watson boasted a rich, expressive voice, and he became a winning performer who was widely admired for his grace, humility and good humor until his death at 89 in May 2012. "He is single-handedly responsible for the extraordinary increase in acoustic flat-picking and fingerpicking guitar performance," declared Smithsonian folklorist Ralph Rinzer, who discovered Watson in 1960. "His flat-picking style has no precedent in earlier country music history." Watson never had a gold record. He just changed the way entire genres of American music are played. ∎

## Andy Griffith
### He spoke softly, and needed no stick

**T**HE ANDY GRIFFITH SHOW WAS A KIND OF work of nostalgia even as it originally aired. Its laconic voice and rural setting were a contrast with the urban settings and wisecracking pace of much of 1950s TV comedy. As Sheriff Andy Taylor, Griffith—in contrast to such popular stars as Lucille Ball and Jackie Gleason—let his co-stars, like Don Knotts, take the comic lead. Sheriff Taylor was the calm, imperturbable sounding board and problem solver who showed that patience and good humor could be the most effective weapons. Griffith, also a producer of the show, modeled the fictional hamlet of Mayberry on his hometown, Mount Airy, N.C. At least in this half-hour of TV, there was no problem that couldn't be solved with plain talk, and maybe some of Aunt Bee's biscuits.

Griffith, who died at 86 in July 2012, enjoyed a late-career comeback with the detective show *Matlock*. Less familiar is his memorable first movie role, as Lonesome Rhodes, the folksy TV host turned demagogue in 1957's *A Face in the Crowd*. Ambitious, insinuating and deceptively populist, Rhodes prefigured the cable-TV manipulators who would come along decades later. In Rhodes and Taylor, Griffith showed the fine line between the best and worst of Americana: how wisdom could be hidden in small-town guilelessness, how wickedness could package itself in a voice as sweet and rich as pecan pie. ∎

Griffith in the 1960s

FROM LEFT: EVERETT COLLECTION; JOHN SPRINGER COLLECTION/CORBIS

**Helm in 1976**

## Levon Helm
### He delved into the roots of rock

LEVON HELM WAS ONE OF THE MOST CEL-ebrated rock drummers of the past 50 years and a vocalist whose raw, red-dirt vocals were unmistakable. He uniquely embodied two sets of folk memories in his music, one of the pop culture of the 1960s, and another of an older, lost America of dirt farmers, train robbers and Civil War veterans scratching out the foundations of the Republic.

Born to a family of farmers in Arkansas in 1940, Mark Lavon ("Levon") Helm started playing with local groups while he was still at school, then joined the band of Ronnie Hawkins, a gifted rockabilly singer. When Hawkins moved to Toronto, Helm went along and joined a group of four local musicians. After backing Bob Dylan, the Band, as the quintet became known, got a recording contract and became one of the seminal groups of the 1960s.

With its first two albums, *Music from Big Pink* and *The Band,* the group pioneered a new genre, roots rock, that was both easy on the ear and rhythmically complex. Driven by Helm's pounding drums and impassioned vocals, the Band's music rocked, rolled and strolled through the cluttered attic of American musical history. In later years, after the Band split up and he was fighting cancer, Helm led a knockout band that played informal "Midnight Rambles" at his house in Woodstock, N.Y. The group's recordings won three Grammy Awards before Helms, 71, succumbed to cancer in April 2012. ■

FROM LEFT: KEN REGAN—CAMERA 5; EVERETT COLLECTION

## Earl Scruggs
### He taught the banjo to dance

YOU COULD THINK OF EARL SCRUGGS as the Doc Watson of the banjo—and both men would be flattered. When Bill Monroe first came up with bluegrass, banjo players used the clawhammer style, flailing hard with their fingers and hands to play chords to create the music's "high, lonesome sound." But when Scruggs, sitting on his porch in Shelby, N.C., grabbed his guitar picks and mastered his rolling, three-finger picking style to create the crisp clusters of twangs we know today, he changed the sound of bluegrass forever.

A self-taught musician, Scruggs shot to prominence after he joined Monroe's Blue Grass Boys in late 1945. In 1948 he and guitarist Lester Flatt formed the Foggy Mountain Boys, later known simply as Flatt and Scruggs. After scoring a novelty hit with *The Ballad of Jed Clampett,* the theme song for TV's *The Beverly Hillbillies,* Flatt and Scruggs won a Grammy Award in 1969 for Scruggs' classic instrumental *Foggy Mountain Breakdown,* whose careening, out-of-control speed drove the soundtrack of the film *Bonnie and Clyde.* By March 2012, when Scruggs died at 88, his fluid picking style was as instantly familiar as Johnny Cash's baritone or Hank Williams' heartbreak. He helped transform a regional sound into a national passion. ■

**Scruggs in 1969**

## Andy Williams
### He was everyone's huckleberry friend

**H**IS RECORDING OF *MOON RIVER* MADE Andy Williams a star, but he was far from a one-hit wonder: he was a performer, and a minor cultural treasure, for three-quarters of a century. The Iowa-born crooner began singing at age 8 with his three older brothers and peaked as a recording artist in the decade from the mid-1950s to the mid-'60s, withstanding the first age of rock and finding a niche as the period's most amiable pop baritone. Williams' pleasant presence, as comfortable as the cashmere sweaters he wore, proved equally suitable for TV: *The Andy Williams Show* charmed and soothed viewers from 1962 to 1971. He ended his career beguiling audiences at his Moon River Theatre in the country-music mecca of Branson, Mo., where he died in September at 84.

## Dick Clark
### He gave rock 'n' roll a makeover

**T**HE WORLD'S OLDEST teenager died in April at 82. Dick Clark left behind a media empire and a legacy as TV's pre-eminent disc jockey and baby-sitter for a generation of kids raised on rock 'n' roll. In 1956, at age 26, he assumed host duties on a Philadelphia afternoon TV show called *Bandstand,* and within years he became an important cultural force. Calming, genial and sweet-faced, he became a canny conduit to spread the social and sonic threat of rock 'n' roll from kids' bedrooms into the nation's living rooms. He hosted TV game shows, produced "reality" series and an Elvis biopic movie, and in 1974 he became the face of New Year's with his annual *New Year's Rockin' Eve* show from Times Square in New York City.

## Marvin Hamlisch
### His melodies captured the way we were

**T**HE UNERRING COMPOSER OF LATE-20TH century romantic standards was a child prodigy, a singular sensation who, at 7, was the youngest musician to be admitted to Juilliard. Ten years later Marvin Hamlisch was playing for Judy Garland and Liza Minnelli; and at 19 he was Barbra Streisand's rehearsal pianist for *Funny Girl.* He was just 29 when he concocted the perfect Streisand ballad, *The Way We Were,* and he would go on to win Oscars, a Grammy, an Emmy, a Tony and a Pulitzer—the last for *A Chorus Line,* his tribute to Broadway's

itinerant gypsies (embodied in the powerful aria *What I Did for Love*).

Hamlisch died at 68 in August; his song for a 1977 Bond movie described his art perfectly: nobody did it better.

## Davy Jones
### A tiny talent made Monkees fans swoon

**A** CUTE, DIMINUTIVE BRIT, DAVY JONES was the member of the made-for-TV band the Monkees who most resembled the classic model of a '60s music heartthrob: English-accented, boy-faced, with a clear singing tone and wide, earnest eyes. The quartet's tambourine-tapping dreamboat and front man, Jones was 66 when he died in February. He sang many of the group's biggest hits, including *Daydream Believer*—though of the songs he fronted on, his favorite was *Valleri.*

Even if *The Monkees* was never meant to be more than fluff and a hit-single generator, we shouldn't sell the show short. It was far better TV than it had to be. Whatever Jones and the Monkees were meant to be, they became creative artists in their own right, and Jones' chipper Brit-pop presence was a big reason they were able to create work that was commercial and wholesome yet at times impressively weird.

CLOCKWISE FROM TOP LEFT: MICHAEL OCHS ARCHIVES/GETTY IMAGES; HULTON-DEUTSCH COLLECTION/CORBIS; RETNA/PHOTOSHOT/EVERETT COLLECTION; AP

CLOCKWISE FROM TOP LEFT: MICHAEL OCHS ARCHIVES/GETTY IMAGES; JOHN SPRINGER COLLECTION/CORBIS; MICHAEL OCHS ARCHIVES—GETTY IMAGES; BEBETO MATTHEWS—AP/CORBIS

## Etta James
### Farewell to a gritty, gutsy, sexy singer

SHE WASN'T JUST A BLUES LEGEND; ETTA James was an icon. With a voice she could mold to belt out delicate ballads like *At Last* and husky, heart-shredding blues hits like *I'd Rather Go Blind,* James, who died in January at 73, won Grammys for her blues and jazz recordings and was inducted into both the Blues and the Rock and Roll halls of fame. "Etta is earthy and gritty," blues singer Bonnie Raitt wrote in *Rolling Stone* in 2005, "ribald and out-there in a way that few performers have the guts to be." Over her nearly six-decade career, James helped construct the bridge between blues and rock 'n' roll. "Etta was my soulmate," Rolling Stones guitarist Keith Richards said. "Never did I see such energy and such a lust for life."

## Leroy Neiman
### He turned sports fans into art lovers

THE PEOPLE THAT LOVE MY PAINTINGS ... they're spectators, not viewers," LeRoy Neiman once said. Those spectators, drawn to his kinetically colored renderings of sporting events, helped make him one of the most popular American artists of the past 50 years. Neiman, who died in June at 91, was the artist-in-residence for the 1969 New York Jets, designed *Playboy's* sultry trademark

"Femlin," sketched the 1972 world chess tournament on live TV and drew boxer Muhammad Ali so many times that the painter devoted a book to the boxer.

## Ernest Borgnine
### He was Hollywood's favorite Everyman

THE SON OF ITALIAN IMMIGRANTS, HE was like the big, boisterous uncle at the family dinner party: a lumpen raconteur who would geyser opinions, reach down the long table for a second helping, impress the kids and annoy prim Aunt Ethel with his booming personality. Millions of these characters exist in America, but there was only one Ernest Borgnine. He served 10 years in the Navy and was in his 30s before his mom suggested he try acting. Hollywood took a look at that meaty face and heavy form and cast him as a prime bully. He broke

out of tough-guy roles to earn an Oscar in 1956 as the lonely butcher in *Marty* and later starred in four seasons of the military sitcom *McHale's Navy.* The definition of a working actor, he appeared in scores of films before his death at 95 in July.

## Donna Summer
### Disco's queen outlasted the '70s

WITH A VOICE THAT COULD RANGE from airy to sultry in the space of a phrase, Donna Summer was the indisputable queen of disco. Born LaDonna Andrea Grimes on Dec. 31, 1948, in Boston, she grew up in a working-class household with six siblings and began singing in a church choir. At age 18 she landed a role in the touring company of *Hair* and moved to Europe with the production. Her breakout came in 1975, with a 17-minute sexy soul groove called *Love to Love You, Baby.* It hit the top of the U.S. charts by 1976.

Summer became disco's reigning diva: her classics include *I Feel Love, Bad Girls, Last Dance* and *She Works Hard for the Money.* She died in May 2012 at 63, following a long battle with cancer.

Diller

## Andrew Breitbart

The gleefully belligerent right-wing blogger, who viewed politics and journalism as contact sports and sometimes hit below the belt, died unexpectedly from heart failure at only 43 in March.

## Hal David

With their composer-lyricist partnership, Burt Bacharach and Hal David reached the pinnacle of romantic popcraft, writing hits for Tom Jones, Dusty Springfield and Dionne Warwick. David, who was 91 when he died on Sept. 1, claimed "Alfie" was his favorite song.

## Phyllis Diller

The mother of five made her debut as a comic at age 38. A pioneer in a man's world, she joked about her home life, her bad driving and her husband—"Fang"—and opened the door for a flock of followers. She died at 95 in August.

## Robin Gibb

One of the Bee Gees, the three brothers who conquered music in both the '60s and the disco era, he was a fine singer and writer in his own right. He died in May at 62.

## Robert Hughes

Widely considered the finest art critic of his era, the veteran TIME writer deployed his discriminating eye and cogent prose to illuminate

modern art (*The Shock of the New,* 1980) and the history of his native Australia (*The Fatal Shore,* 1987). He died in August at 74.

## Thomas Kinkade

The "painter of light" created warm, romantic pastel scenes that millions loved, but critics called kitschy. Sadly, he also harbored a dark side, and his death at 54 in April was attributed to substance abuse.

## Sun Myung Moon

The South Korean preacher, who died in September at 93, drove the expansion of his Unification Church, became very wealthy, and served a brief term in the U.S. for tax evasion. He also staged spectacular mass rituals in which thousands of couples were wed at once.

## Ferdinand A. Porsche

He designed the Porsche 911 in 1963; with its flyline roof and headlights fitted into front wings flanking a low hood, it became a style icon. The grandson of the founder of Porsche died in April at 76.

## Junior Seau

Ferocious on the field, 12-time Pro Bowl linebacker Seau was likable, thoughtful and charitable off it. He died at 43 in April by shooting himself in the chest, perhaps to preserve his brain for evidence of concussion-related ailments.

Porsche

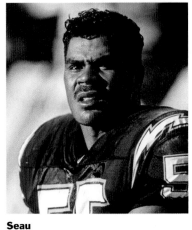

Seau

## Norodom Sihanouk

A ruthless politician (and a tireless playboy), King Sihanouk reigned over Cambodia during a frenzied period of war and turmoil. He was living in exile in Beijing when the Khmer Rouge conducted a bloody reign of terror in his nation. He died in October at age 90.

## Arlen Specter

The 30-year GOP Senator from Pennsylvania was an abrasive moderate who played key roles in selecting Supreme Court Justices and in passing Obama Administration bills. He became a Democrat in 2009 but did not keep his Senate seat. He died in October at 82.

## Arthur Ochs Sulzberger

Taking over the family business—the New York *Times*—in 1963, he refreshed and enlarged its form and coverage and won a major victory for freedom of the press with the publication of the Pentagon Papers in 1971. He died at 86 in September.

## Adam Yauch

Yes, the Beastie Boy fought for your right to party. But he also fought, with passion and perserverance, for the rights of Tibetans. A serious, compassionate thinker, he was only 47 when he died of cancer in May.

CLOCKWISE FROM TOP LEFT: KEN WHITMORE—MPTVIMAGES; GREG TROTT—AP; PORSCHE/ZUMA PRESS

Mokena Community
Public Library District

3 1985 00249 6227